Twayne's United States Authors Series

Sylvia E. Bowman, *Editor*

INDIANA UNIVERSITY

Winston Churchill

WINSTON CHURCHILL

by **WARREN I. TITUS**

George Peabody College for Teachers

(TUSAS) 43

Twayne Publishers, Inc.   ::   New York

To My Mother
AND
For My Wife

Preface

THE MAJOR AUTHORS of a literary era often stand outside their own political and cultural times. Universal in scope and interest, they may not reflect contemporary popular moods in those works that frequently take on greatest critical significance. The writings of authors of lesser stature, on the other hand, usually do indicate the prevailing temper of the day and generally mirror the age from which they derive. For this reason, minor authors are frequently more accurate indicators of popular reading taste and interest than their major contemporaries who tower over them in literary worth.

Such an author was the American Winston Churchill, whose versatile career as a public figure spanned the years of the Progressive era at the turn of the twentieth century. Churchill was a novelist, essayist, historian, and political figure during that exciting era in this country when many highly successful writers were caught up in the Rooseveltian enthusiasms of the moment. From 1899 to 1916, Churchill was probably the author most widely read by the American middle class. His audience frequently shared his interests and his concerns as it read and discussed his books and his career in Progressive politics.

It is the principal intent of this study to show how Churchill's literary works mirrored the issues that occupied the American popular mind during the years of his greatest acclaim. I have not attempted to write a biography; only those facts of the man's life have been given which seemed necessary to lend some structure and unity to the book or which shed some light on those writing interests manifested at any particular moment in his time.

Since Churchill's novels are seldom read today (most of them have long been out of print), it has seemed advisable to summarize the content of each. Generous samples of contemporary critical reviews have also been included to show further the author's impact on his own day. That Churchill has faded rather completely from the current literary scene would seem to be a self-evident truth. Yet, an examination of the popular literary and political record of the first two decades of the century indicates immediately that he was an author who enjoyed a tremendous vogue and whose ideas were taken seriously by that generation immersed in the Progressive mold. As such, he is a figure worthy of study by today's student of American civilization.

I am primarily indebted to Professor Oscar Cargill, Chairman of the Department of English, Graduate School of Arts and Science, New York University, for stimulating and guiding my initial interest in Churchill. Sylvia Bowman, editor of Twayne's United States Authors Series, gave sound advice and helpful editorial assistance in the preparation of the present work. Most of the factual information about Churchill comes from published contemporary accounts in newspapers and magazines. However, George Brett, Jr., George Rublee, Upton Sinclair, Anthony Montague Browne (Secretary to Sir Winston S. Churchill), Corinne Tennyson Davids, David Arnold Balch, J. Owen Grundy, Robert von Nardroff, Vera Russell, and John S. Mayfield, some of whom either knew Winston Churchill personally or corresponded with him, contributed in one way or another to my further understanding of the man and his works.

Librarians at the following institutions were helpful in making available their resources for my use: Missouri Historical Society Library, St. Louis Public Library, the Library of Congress, the Navy Section of the United States National Archives, the Library of the United States Naval Academy, New York Public Library, Boston Public Library, and the Joint University Libraries of Nashville, Tennessee. Indeed, my literary debts are great; but I hasten to add that whatever inaccuracies or deficiencies the book may contain are solely my responsibility.

Finally, it should be noted that without the encouragement and forbearance of my family this study could not have been completed.

WARREN I. TITUS

George Peabody College
  for Teachers

Acknowledgments

Grateful acknowledgment is made to the following publishers and authors:

To Appleton-Century-Crofts for permission to quote from Fred Lewis Pattee's *The New American Literature*, and from Arthur H. Quinn's *The Literature of the American People*, copyright 1951.

To Mrs. Anne Van Doren Ross, Mrs. Margaret Bevans, and Mrs. Barbara Klaw for permission to quote from Carl Van Doren's *Contemporary American Novelists, 1900-1920*.

To the Macmillan Company for permission to quote from Carl Van Doren's *The American Novel*, copyright 1940.

To Harcourt, Brace and World, Inc. for permission to quote from Henry F. Pringle's *Theodore Roosevelt: A Biography* and Vernon L. Parrington's *Main Currents in American Thought*.

To Alfred A. Knopf, Inc. for permission to quote from Richard Hofstadter's *The American Political Tradition and the Men Who Made It*, and from H. L. Mencken's *Prejudices, Fourth Series*.

To Richard Hofstadter for permission to quote from his *The Age of Reform: From Bryan to F.D.R.*

To the *American Historical Review* for permission to quote from Arthur S. Link's "What Happened to the Progressive Movement in the 1920's," which appeared in the July, 1959, issue.

To *Hobbies* magazine and Mr. Cyril Clemens for permission to quote from "A Visit With the American Winston Churchill," which appeared in the May, 1947, issue.

To the Pennsylvania State University Press for permission to quote from Fred L. Pattee's *Penn State Yankee*, copyright 1953.

To the University of Michigan Press for permission to quote from Charles C. Walcutt's *The Romantic Compromise in the Novels of Winston Churchill*, copyright 1951.

To E. P. Dutton and Co., Inc. for permission to quote from Van Wyck Brooks's *The Confident Years, 1885-1915*.

To Harvard University Press for permission to quote from Elting E. Morison's *The Letters of Theodore Roosevelt*.

To the Ronald Press Company for permission to quote from Ralph H. Babriel's *The Course of American Democratic Thought*, copyright 1940.

To Alfred Kazin for permission to quote from his *On Native Grounds* (Reynal and Co., 1942).

To Mrs. Phoebe Grace Storms for permission to quote from her unpublished master's thesis, *Winston Churchill: A Critical Study*, Southern Methodist University, 1941.

Contents

Chronology

1871   Winston Churchill born November 10, in St. Louis, Missouri, the only child of Edward Spaulding and Emma Bell Churchill. Mother dies within three weeks. Winston adopted by the James B. Gazzams, his aunt and uncle on the maternal side.

1879   Enters Smith Academy, a preparatory school connected with Washington University.

1888   Graduates from Smith Academy on June 12.

1890   Is appointed a Naval Cadet at United States Naval Academy in Annapolis on May 21.

1894   Graduates from Naval Academy in June. Assigned to cruiser *San Francisco* at the New York Navy Yard. Resignation as a Naval Cadet accepted as of September 11. Appointed naval editor of *Army and Navy Journal* in late September.

1895   Accepts position with *Cosmopolitan* where he eventually becomes managing editor. Resigns position in the autumn to take up a writing career. Moves to Irvington-on-the-Hudson, New York. Marries Mabel Harlakenden Hall of St. Louis on October 22.

1896   April 25, Churchill sails for Europe leaving manuscript of *The Celebrity* with Albert Shaw. "Mr. Keegan's Elopement" published in June in *Century* magazine. Starts work on *Richard Carvel*. Journeys south to Washington, Annapolis, and Baltimore during the winter of 1896-97 to get background material for the novel.

1897   Daughter Mabel born. Rewrites *The Celebrity* twice at Lake George, New York. Works on *Richard Carvel* at St. Louis during autumn and winter of 1897-98.

1898   *The Celebrity* published in January; "Admiral Dewey: A Character Sketch," in *Review of Reviews* in June; "By Order of the Admiral: A Story of the Times," in *Century* magazine, July; "Battle with Cervera's Fleet Off Santiago," in *Review of Reviews*, August. Moves to South Nyack, New York.

1899　*Richard Carvel* published in June. Buys one-hundred acres of land overlooking the Connecticut River valley in Cornish, New Hampshire. Moves there in the summer.

1900　Successful stage version of *Richard Carvel* is produced in New York and by touring road company. Meets Winston Spencer Churchill at a dinner in Boston in December.

1901　*The Crisis* published in May. Speaks at the dedication of the Louisiana Purchase Building at the Pan-American Exposition in Buffalo, New York, during the summer. Makes acquaintance of Theodore Roosevelt. Six-month tour of Europe during autumn and winter.

1902　Highly successful New York and road company productions of *The Crisis*. Churchill elected Cornish representative in New Hampshire legislature in November.

1903　Churchill unsuccessfully introduces reform bills into the New Hampshire legislature. Tours the Mississippi Valley and the South to gather material for *The Crossing*. Son John born.

1904　*The Crossing* published in May to coincide with St. Louis World's Fair Exposition celebrating the Louisiana Purchase. June 21-23, attends Republican Convention in Chicago as a New Hampshire delegate in support of Theodore Roosevelt. Is re-elected to a second term in the state legislature.

1905　Second session in the state legislature where he begins a conflict with Boston and Maine Railroad domination of the state.

1906　*The Title-Mart,* "an Anglo-American comedy by Winston Churchill," opens at the Madison Square Theater in New York on February 20. Closes after two weeks. Similar disappointing productions take place later the same year in Washington, Philadelphia, and Boston. *Coniston* published in June, based partly on Churchill's political experience. Is nominated by the Lincoln Republican Club to seek the Republican nomination for Governor of New Hampshire. Is defeated for the nomination largely because of railroad opposition.

1907   Acts as part-time lobbyist for various reform measures at Concord.

1908   *Mr. Crewe's Career* published in May. Stumps the state for William Howard Taft's nomination and election.

1909   Sails for Europe for a tour that was to take him as far as Egypt.

1910   *A Modern Chronicle* published in March.

1911   Addresses the Seabury Conference of the Episcopal Church in Cambridge, Massachusetts, in July.

1912   "Modern Government and Christianity" published in the *Atlantic* in January. "Winston Churchill's Christian Anarchism" published in *Current Literature* in February. Son Creighton born. *The Inside of the Cup* serialized in *Hearst's* magazine beginning in May. "A Matter for the Individual to Settle" published in *Hearst's* magazine in June. Runs and is defeated for Governor of New Hampshire on the Progressive Party ticket. Spends winter of 1912-13 in Berkeley, California.

1913   *The Inside of the Cup* published in March; "Our Common-Sense Marriages" in *Good Housekeeping* in July. Speaks at Pacific Theological Seminary and University of California in spring. Delivers a series of religious lectures from pulpits of the West Coast. "The Modern Quest for Religion" in *Century* magazine in December. Summers, 1913 and 1914, rents "Harlakenden House" to Woodrow Wilson as a summer White House. Lives for a time at Santa Barbara and Lake Tahoe, California. Is elected President of Author's League of America.

1914   Churchill lectures at Harvard, Columbia, and Union Theological Seminary in the spring. Returns to New England in autumn. *A Far Country* serialized in *Hearst's* beginning in March.

1915   *A Far Country* published in June.

1916   "A Plea for the American Tradition" published in *Harper's* in January. Attends Progressive Party Convention as observer; writes his impressions in "Roosevelt and His Friends," *Collier's*, July 8. *The Dwelling-Place of Light* begins serialization in *Hearst's* during the summer. Gives addresses at Yale on "Some Religious Paradoxes in Democracy" and at Wellesley on "The Religious Theory of Democracy."

1917 "A Call to the Marine Corps" appears in New York *Times* on June 14; "Naval Organization, American and British," *Atlantic*, August; "The Faith of Frances Craniford" written and published for Episcopal Church Pension Fund. *The Dwelling-Place of Light* published in October. Tours the war fronts at the invitation of Josephus Daniels, Secretary of the Navy; visits France, Britain, and Ireland.

1918 Observations on the war fronts appear in *Scribner's* magazine for February, March, and April; *A Traveller in War-Time* published in July; pamphlet, "St. Louis After the War," published in December. (Introduction to the pamphlet published as an article in *American City* in January, 1919.)

1919 *Dr. Jonathan* published in September.

1922 "Two Minds for One" published in New York *Times Book Review and Magazine*, March 26; "The Knowledge of Good and Evil" in *North American Review* in April; "An Uncharted Way" in *Yale Review*, April.

1923 "Harlakenden House," Churchill's Cornish home, destroyed by fire.

1940 *The Uncharted Way* published by Dorrance & Company. (The only Churchill book not published by Macmillan.)

1945 Mrs. Churchill dies in May.

1947 Churchill dies in March at Winter Park, Florida. Is buried in Cornish, New Hampshire.

Winston Churchill

CHAPTER *1*

The Early Years

IN THE LATE AUTUMN of 1900, a young English war
correspondent fresh from an exciting chase-and-escape experience in the Boer War was entertained "at a very gay banquet
of young men" in Boston. His host for the occasion was an
illustrious American novelist who bore his name and with whom
he had previously engaged in some limited correspondence.[1]
The dinner-meeting, replete with complimentary speeches and
the usual exchange of amenities, marked the confluence of two
rising personalities who were even then being confused in the
public mind and who were to become a part of the annals of
popular history during the next decades of the twentieth century.

In 1900, Winston Spencer Churchill, the young English war
correspondent, had only the beginnings of a secure reputation.
Winston Churchill, the American novelist, on the other hand,
was enjoying a newly acquired recognition that made him well
known to a large reading public in America and abroad. It was
small wonder that the younger Englishman, who had inclinations
for a writing career himself, should search out what he termed
"the other Richmond in the field" on his arrival in the United
States.

Over the next two decades, the American was to thrill his
reading audience time and again with best-sellers, was to thrust
himself into the maelstrom of Progressive politics, and was to
taper off an active life with a zeal for social and religious
reform that added luster to his popular acclaim. A barometer of
public reading taste and an epitome of the ideals of the American Progressive, the American Churchill was to win an even
more enviable place for himself in the coming years of the
century, and then was to drop out of the public eye, leaving
behind a literary legacy of recorded segments of American life.

I

It was appropriate, perhaps, that Winston Churchill, as a recorder of the American historical and political scene, should have had a distinguished ancestry. Both the Churchills and the Blaines could boast some proud names in their genealogy. The American author's remote ancestor, John Churchill, came originally from Dorsetshire in England and settled in Plymouth, Massachusetts, as early as 1641. A nearer and more direct ancestor, Robert Churchill, captained the first privateer of the American Revolution, sailing out of Plymouth to prey on enemy shipping. Churchill's own branch of the family moved later to Portland, Maine, where it went into the West India trade. On his mother's side, through the Blaines, he was descended from John Dwight, the founder of Dedham, Massachusetts, and from Jonathan Edwards, the Puritan intellectual giant of the eighteenth century.[2]

His New England ancestry was always important for Churchill, but equally important was his Western birth. For he was a product of the westward movement—of two streams of it that converged in St. Louis toward the middle of the nineteenth century. His mother's family had migrated into Virginia, thence to Kentucky, and finally to St. Louis; there it met the other New England stream, the Churchills, in the person of Winston's own father, Edward.

Edward Spaulding Churchill, son of a prominent merchant in the West India trade, was born in Portland, Maine, on April 2, 1846. After engaging for a time in the sugar business in Cuba, Edward Churchill journeyed west in 1870 to St. Louis where it would seem he never intended to take root but where he met and married Emma Bell Blaine, daughter of John L. and Margaret D. Blaine. The marriage was destined to be short-lived, for Emma Churchill died within three weeks after a son, Winston, was born on November 10, 1871.

Winston Churchill, therefore, never knew his mother. But Emma Bell Blaine was the direct inheritor of a proud tradition. Her father had been a member of a famous Virginia-Kentucky family, and her mother was a near relative of the John Bell of Tennessee who was a candidate for President of the United States on the Constitutional Unionist ticket in 1860. By all accounts she was a woman of charm, beauty, and intellect.

[20]

As for the father, he drifted out of his son's life shortly after he saw the infant adopted by his wife's sister and her husband, the James B. Gazzams of St. Louis. The Gazzams were to be parents to young Churchill in everything but fact. They nursed him, reared him, educated him, and generally provided the only home and family he knew until he left their household to go to Annapolis in 1890. It is noteworthy, however, that Churchill never forgot his factual state of orphanage—a condition that curiously tinged in a minor way some of his earliest attempts at fiction.

II

Life in St. Louis in the 1870's and the 1880's seems to have proved pleasant enough to the youthful Churchill. He gloried in the old city beside the river—a city that had seen the successive waves of immigration, that had grown westward away from the Mississippi banks, and that bore the mark of heterogeneity that was to impress him always. At a later time, he was to comment, "I used to think that the residential districts of the city, with their graceful overhanging trees, were the most beautiful I had even seen. And I do not mean this as idle flattery. I still think that there is a group of early families here which stands for the best there is in America. Their culture, their ideals, their family life, has a unique charm that I have never found surpassed in any part of the country."[3] Churchill reflected in this reaction the love of the romantic and the concern with the stateliness of good living that were to haunt the historical novels and to govern his personal life when he sought his own home.

School for Churchill was Smith Academy, a preparatory school connected with Washington University. His earliest memories of academic life went back to Smith. He was seven years old when he first entered the academy in September of 1879. Well liked by his fellow students and by the teachers from the start, young Churchill was a good student who liked books well enough; but he was not considered a genius—or scarcely a potential, successful novelist, although he always did well in language. Charles Curd, one of his teachers at Smith, speaking of his later work in mathematics (after Winston had decided to enter the navy), reported that he applied himself very closely and that his work in mathematics was "almost perfect." But he added, "I never expected him to attain fame in the way that he has, because in his school days he didn't strike me as having the necessary application for constant literary work."[4] He was graduated from the academy on June 12, 1888, when sixteen years of age.

During his early youth and adolescence, Churchill had as classmates and playmates sons and daughters of some of the prominent families in St. Louis. Some of these connections were later to be fictionalized in his novels—particularly in *The Crisis* and in *A Modern Chronicle* where St. Louis scenes are dominant. There the proud, dignified, reasonable life that young Churchill saw around him is painted with the loving care of a nostalgic dreamer. To the eye of a stranger, St. Louis in the 1880's may have been ugly. But to Churchill it was a beautiful city, and he never lost his love for it.

III

Graduation from Smith Academy found young Churchill without immediate funds for a college education. It is possible that he could have attended Washington University, to which Smith Academy was attached. But the cost, though small, would probably have been prohibitive. As it was, he had to work to help pay his way in the Gazzam household. Consequently, when opportunity came for an education at government expense, Churchill was quick to accept.[5] Through F. G. Niedringhaus, congressman from the Eighth Congressional District of Missouri, he received an appointment to the United States Naval Academy in May, 1890, and reported that same summer as a Naval Cadet (a title then given to midshipmen) at Annapolis.[6]

Churchill quickly adjusted to naval routine. The record of his Annapolis career is an excellent one. He started with mathematics, English, French, and German. As he approached graduation year, technical courses replaced the work in languages. Churchill did well in all of them. It is significant, however, that he consistently stood better in languages than in the sciences; his work in English, French, and German was superior at all times.[7]

Though some had called him a bookish lad back in St. Louis, he turned increasingly to athletics at Annapolis. He did not play on the regular football team, but he played right guard on the champion inter-class team. Fencing was a new sport for him, an exciting activity that was to give him some useful material for *Richard Carvel*. But rowing was the sport in which he excelled. He was directly responsible for its revival at Annapolis, an accomplishment that he always viewed with the greatest pride.

In addition to several lasting friendships made at the academy, Churchill came to know numerous people in the town of Annapolis. He fell in love with the place and was delighted to roam its historic streets and to visit in the charming homes of the citizens, many of whom were direct descendants of the first settlers. Indeed, the influence of the old colonial city with its mansions, its narrow streets, and its gay social life was to be directly responsible for Churchill's first great literary success: much of *Richard Carvel* came directly from the author's Annapolis experience.

Although Churchill always wrote with great pride and something of pleasant nostalgia when describing his navy days in later years, it is doubtful that he ever intended to make a career of the navy.[8] Annapolis was but a means to an education, a passing interlude in a life that had already begun to foreshadow itself before he left the academy. When an interviewer from the Boston *Herald* asked him in 1899 when he first decided he wanted to write novels, he replied, "I knew before I left Annapolis."[9]

Under the influence of Commander Craig of the English department, Churchill had turned to writing fiction during his later cadet days. Craig thought the young man had some talent and encouraged him.[10] Churchill's early love for and ability in languages further turned him in that direction; in addition, his interest in the nation's history was whetted by the Naval Academy life. Always one who had a love for the romantic past, the St. Louis youth had delighted in hearing the tales of the old Civil War veterans; he had loved to wander in the historic spots of the city along the Mississippi; he had learned the stories of the city's origins. At Annapolis, this interest was increased. There is no record that he took any history courses at the academy, but the life there would naturally turn the thoughts of such a youth toward the nation's great past. Much of the ardent patriotism that appears in the historical novels was due to this influence.

In June, 1894, young Churchill graduated from the United States Naval Academy. He was immediately assigned to the cruiser *San Francisco,* then at New York harbor. For three months he remained on the *San Francisco,* occasionally cruising in Long Island Sound, but most of the time tied up at the New York navy yard. Life on a becalmed cruiser was scarcely appealing. New York was near, and there was the lure of possible opportunity in the field of journalism where he could indulge his new interest in writing. As early as August 3, 1894, he addressed the Secretary of the Navy, asking for a five-week leave of absence beginning on August 6 and requesting that his resignation be accepted at the expiration of that time. Such was established procedure in the naval service of 1894. His request was granted; his resignation as a Naval Cadet was accepted to take effect on September 11, 1894.[11]

IV

Churchill was not long in finding employment in New York. Late in September, 1894, he went to work for the *Army and Navy Journal* and began his brief career in journalism. His duties with the publication—now defunct but then largely a service journal devoted to glorification of the military life— were at first largely routine. Later, he attained the position of naval editor because of his experience at the academy. More important, his brief period with the journal served as a useful apprenticeship for a better job in the magazine world.

In the spring of 1895, Churchill took a position with *Cosmopolitan* where he eventually found himself managing editor. Despite his success in journalism, however, Churchill soon discovered that editorial tasks irked him. He had fully decided he wanted to write fiction. The *Cosmopolitan,* on the other hand, wanted a magazine editor who would devote full time to his duties. The two interests conflicted. Consequently, when he achieved other sure means of financial support through marriage in the fall of 1895, he resigned his position with the magazine to engage in the full-time work of a creative novelist.

Churchill's marriage to Mabel Harlakenden Hall on October 22, 1895, was not a spontaneous thing; he had known her since

St. Louis days. A young woman of some substance and bearing, Mabel Hall came from an old St. Louis family, the locally famous James E. Yeatman being one of her relatives. Her father had made a small fortune in the iron business, and she was the heiress to a considerable portion of that fortune. Moreover, a woman of enterprise and courage, she could, no doubt, have taken care of herself even in the man's world of 1895.

The wedding took place at "Bellegarde," the old Beverly Allen home in St. Louis, a landmark in local history where Mabel Hall's forebears had been married. As an ante-bellum home, "Bellegarde" was worthy of attention. Churchill used it later as a setting in *The Crisis*.[12]

During the winter of 1895-96, Churchill plunged with his full capacities into the new tasks of creative composition. He had earlier started an historical novel of the American Revolution; he put this aside to write something in a completely different vein—a light satire much in the manner of some contemporary celebrities in the field of fiction. By spring, he had finished the major portion of this novel—a first effort, groping and tentative. On April 25, 1896, the Churchills set sail for Europe on a trip that was to be, in one sense, their honeymoon voyage. Churchill left, for safe keeping, the manuscript of his partially completed work, *The Celebrity*, with a newly acquired friend, Albert Shaw, founder and editor of the *Review of Reviews*. Before Churchill returned from Europe in midsummer of 1896, the Macmillan Company had expressed interest in the book.

Churchill's initial connection with the publishing house of Macmillan was largely engineered by Shaw. In April, 1896, George Brett, president of the Macmillan Company, did not know Churchill, but he did know Albert Shaw as an able, scholarly editor. Shaw, a great inspiration to scores of young authors, gave encouragement wherever he could; and his intervention in Churchill's behalf at the right time launched Churchill successfully on his writing career.[13]

When Churchill sailed for Europe, he had considered *The Celebrity* as "sort of an overture—just a first flight, to test my writing strength."[14] After Churchill had sailed, Shaw gave the manuscript to George Brett, who read the uncompleted novel, liked it, and declared that he would publish it if the second half proved to be as good as the first.

Shaw immediately got in contact with Churchill, who was by then enjoying the historic and picturesque attractions of Europe. The news so encouraged Churchill that he buckled down in the midst of the vacation trip and wrote the final portions of the novel which he forwarded to the publisher. When he met George Brett, Brett said, "If you will take my advice you will continue to rewrite this manuscript until I accept it."[15] Churchill took the advice, but he laid the manuscript aside until the following summer in order to work on another, more extensive historical novel he had been dallying with since the Annapolis days. But the introduction to Brett was made; and, as it turned out, a long-lasting publisher-author relationship had been inaugurated.

V

Meanwhile, in June, 1896, Churchill for the first time burst into print with his fiction when *Century* magazine published one of his earliest stories, "Mr. Keegan's Elopement." A trivial work in which he made use of naval jargon and navy personalities he had met in service, none of the characters is alive and the plot is obvious from the first. Churchill himself never took the story seriously, and it must have been a source of some embarrassment when Macmillan published it in book form in 1903 in the series "Little Novels by Favorite Authors." The only significance it could have borne for him was that it was his first published effort.

In the autumn of 1896, Churchill again put *The Celebrity* aside temporarily, for he was still more interested in his ambitious historical work about the Revolution. He had outlined this novel to Brett, who encouraged him to continue with it, but who also thought *The Celebrity* should be published first in order to get Churchill's name before the reading public. Nonetheless, in the fall and winter of 1896-97, Churchill immersed himself in gathering data for his Revolutionary War novel. Though living on the Hudson, he made frequent journeys south to Washington, Annapolis, and Baltimore to gather information for the story. During one of his visits, he stayed in the charming old "Paca House" directly across the street from the Naval Academy. He roamed again through the old town and revisited many of the people he had met when he had lived in Annapolis. The experience was indicative of the type of painstaking, patient research he was to make such a specialty in all his historical writing.

It was not until the summer of 1897 that Churchill returned to the labors of redoing *The Celebrity*, a task he had been postponing for over a year. Momentarily forgetting history for satire, he rewrote the novel twice in the space of two months. Brett immediately accepted the final version when he saw it later in the summer; the work was copyrighted late in 1897, and the first edition appeared in January, 1898.

Churchill had also sent the first fifty pages of his historical novel to Brett along with *The Celebrity*. Brett liked that too, and an arrangement was made for publication of *Richard Carvel* at the same time that *The Celebrity* was accepted. In the trials of writing *The Celebrity*, Churchill probably learned a valuable lesson—that acceptable literature is born of many revisions. All his works after *The Celebrity* were re-written several times before they achieved final form, and his remarkable persistence in revising was noted in the literary journals.

VI

Although at the time Churchill did not consider *The Celebrity* a major work, he later looked back on it with pride and with more real affection than he displayed for some of his more serious attempts. He remarked on one occasion that it had more of himself in it than any other of his books, although he was not taking himself seriously when he wrote it.[16]

The novel was probably written under the influence of the Van Bibber stories of Richard Harding Davis, which featured a rich young clubman of New York named Courtlandt Van Bibber who reflected both the vices and the virtues of the wealthy social set. Published in 1892, *Van Bibber and Others* had enjoyed a tremendous popularity for a time. Fred Lewis Pattee has reported that the stories "seemed to come from an authority, one who knew to the full the life of the idle rich in the Four Hundred circle of New York. . . . It was good Sunday newspaper stuff and it fed the lean readers of its day."[17] Churchill not only recognized the vogue of these stories but also saw in them something that was appealing: an amusing commentary on a class of people that he was being introduced to increasingly.

So he tried a Van Bibber type in *The Celebrity.* As might have
been expected, Churchill was accused of satirizing Richard
Harding Davis in his novel. Although he denied this most
vehemently, there can be little doubt that something of the
meteoric rise of young Davis must have been in Churchill's mind
as he wrote. His hero is too much like the celebrated journalist
to be completely the product of Churchill's imagination.

The Celebrity is a social satire on the ways of inflated preten-
sion and the idle rich. It is the story of a celebrated author
who seeks to elude a doting public by assuming the disguise of
another man and by journeying west to a summer resort in a
"thriving town near one of the Great Lakes" (probably in
Wisconsin).[18] He is something of a lady's man as well as a
writer; indeed, his writing appeal is largely to a female audience
which lionizes him. Although part of this appeal is the way
he always upholds the sanctity of womanhood in his novels,
his personal life is something else again. No sooner has this
"Celebrity" appeared on the scene of the smart summer resort
in the West, than he proceeds to leave a string of broken hearts
behind him.

His foppishness, his insincerity, and his buoyant egotism are
sources of annoyance to the narrator of the story, a man named
Crocker. Crocker discovers that the "Celebrity" is masquerading
as Charles Wrexell Allen, treasurer of the Miles Standish Bicycle
Company. He sees interesting possibilities for unmasking the
"Celebrity" when it is discovered that the real Allen has
absconded with $100,000 belonging to the company, is now
wanted by the police, and has supposedly headed west.

A series of ridiculous situations results when the "Celebrity"
tries to explain that he really is not Charles Wrexell Allen but
the celebrated author of *The Sybarites.* Crocker knows he is
telling the truth, but he proceeds to embarrass the "Celebrity"
by refusing to back up his story. A Miss Thorn, one of the young
ladies with whom the "Celebrity" has trifled, also knows the
truth, but she resolves to play the game with Crocker. The
"Celebrity," hard pressed to escape the law, is finally deposited
on the Canadian side of what seems to be Lake Superior after a
hilarious chase across the lake in which he is thoroughly
humiliated—much to the great delight of Crocker and Miss
Thorn. Years later, the two of them, now man and wife, encounter

the "Celebrity" in a Paris hotel and discover that he has recovered his equilibrium and is up to his old tricks again. Incidentally, "he is still writing books of a high moral tone and unapproachable principle, and his popularity is undiminished. I have not heard, however, that he has given way to any more whims."[19]

The plot of *The Celebrity* is trivial. Through it all the pose works both ways, for Charles Wrexell Allen escapes by assuming the disguise of the "Celebrity." From first to last, the narrative is farce. Churchill was having fun; he was trying his hand at writing something he thought would amuse his readers. In this respect, at least, he accomplished his purpose, for the novel did capture some public attention. It was reprinted twice in March of 1898; again in May, July, August, September, and October, 1898; and in June, 1899. Other editions came out periodically over the years.

When the reviewers got around to noticing *The Celebrity*, they were divided about its merits. Many reviews were favorable, particularly those written after Churchill had scored with *Richard Carvel*. But there were unfavorable reviews, too, many of which considered the book a slipshod, hasty piece of work. Certainly, the book has some dullness. It is hard to see today how it could have been as popular as it was in 1898—another indication of the changing whims of public fancy!

Mediocre as *The Celebrity* is as fiction, it is noteworthy in Churchill's career as a writer for several reasons. In the first place, it set the pattern for the role Churchill was inadvertently to play all through his career. Never a pioneer in fiction, he was a participant in prevailing popular currents and trends. His novels clearly serve as cultural barometers of what the American public at large was reading between 1898 and 1918, and *The Celebrity* is the first work to reflect this. Richard Harding Davis' success in the Van Bibber series has been noted. This was a "young man's epoch," as Van Wyck Brooks has said.[20]

The fashionable world of New York was depicted by Charles Dana Gibson, creator of the Gibson girl, another symbol of the era. And Gibson was indicative of the times. Brooks comments that "his theme was society in all its phases, horse-shows, weddings and dinner-parties, with the brownstone palaces and the chateaus of Fifth Avenue for settings. . . . They were the sights that charmed Booth Tarkington, the young writer from Indianapolis who arrived in the middle nineties with a novel in his trunk, prepared to admire the long procession of romantically elegant ladies with glitteringly harnessed horses driving in the park."[21] Churchill came to the city directly from the Naval Academy. No doubt, he, too, had read his Davis and observed his Gibson. And he was not inexperienced in the ways of society —for St. Louis also had its "romantically elegant ladies" and its "glitteringly harnessed horses driving in the park." *The Celebrity* is a belated work in the very vein of social satire that was already beginning to fade when Churchill's book was published. He caught the last moments of the fad, but it remains typical of such fiction. A few years later, Edith Wharton was to picture a similar world of fashion much more effectively, but she did not originate the genre.

The Celebrity is significant, in the second place, because Churchill employed the first-person point of view in the book. It was a device that worked reasonably well, and he was to try it in his larger project, the historical novel *Richard Carvel*. There it was not so effective. He returned to it in *The Crossing* without success, whereupon he abandoned first-person narrative for ten years.

Another item of significance about *The Celebrity* is the characterization of Farquahar Fenelon Cooke, a prominent Eastern businessman. In general, the characterization in the book is poor. No memorable people emerge from its pages unless one excepts Cooke—and he, if not really good, is at least alive. More significantly, he is Churchill's first attempt to portray the business tycoon. Although Cooke plays a minor role in the book—he is scarcely more than a side-show character—he is representative, apparently, of what Churchill thought one type of businessman to be. In later works, he was to picture the business executive in unflattering terms; and these portraits are foreshadowed in the depiction of Cooke as a good-natured buffoon. Furthermore, a wealthy man himself, Cooke is the victim of big business, a railroad that is about to fleece him out of some of his Western land—again a suggestion of Churchill's work several years later.

Inelegant, boisterous, profane, friendly, dull, Cooke is the type of Rotary Club bourgeois that Sinclair Lewis was to portray in George Babbitt, except that Cooke has more money. In a sense, Farquahar Fenelon Cooke is Babbitt before Babbitt's day. Churchill was toying with something in this characterization that he might have developed more profitably. As it was, he dropped it until his political phase came along—and even then he was interested in other issues than the idle rich as such.

Another interesting minor figure in *The Celebrity* is Mr. Trevor, an Ohio state senator and the father of one of the young ladies with whom the "Celebrity" flirted. Mr. Trevor is pictured as a bombastic old windbag. He speaks with sweeps of the arm that "he had doubtless learned in the Ohio State Senate," and he is "both a self-made man and a Western politician."[22] This is a prophetic portrait in view of Churchill's later experiences with Eastern self-made men and his depiction of politicians of the New Hampshire legislature.

As for the women characters in the novel, they are portraits that might have been taken directly from Gibson's drawings. They are types Churchill was to repeat in later novels in which the glorification of American womanhood is frequently implied.

The satire—effective in its time but outdated today—is directed against people who go to the summer "watering places" and boarding houses. There is a group of Eastern socialites called "The Ten" who go west to the resort of Asquith and engage in one long round of dances and parties. There is a smaller group called "The Four" that is even more representative and more obnoxious. Significantly, the reader never learns their individual names; they are nonentities who conform to type. They do not work; they effuse charm and delightful conversation; they are decorative; sport is about their only expenditure of energy—horse racing is their particular favorite. Later, Churchill was to move occasionally in similar social circles himself, those very circles that he mildly amuses himself with in the story.

All in all, *The Celebrity* is not a great book. "Only a comedy in book form," Churchill called it in 1899.[23] But it put an unknown author before the public and paved the way for his larger work which was soon to come. Publication of *The Celebrity*, as George Brett had foreseen, made certain that the author of *Richard Carvel* would not be completely unknown to the American reading public.

CHAPTER 2

The Historian

I

WINSTON CHURCHILL always had a great love for history. The aftermath of the Civil War was still strong in St. Louis when Churchill was a boy there, and Civil War lore, in particular, was something he feasted on in those days. As noted earlier, his interest in American history was increased at Annapolis. The old town, the traditions of the naval service, indeed, some of the instruction at the academy nurtured his fondness for the past.[1] Furthermore, in the 1890's, when Churchill first considered writing as a possible career, public reading interest often centered around historical fiction. Perhaps it was natural, then, that Winston Churchill, when he first thought of writing, thought of history. Before he left Annapolis, he had planned *Richard Carvel*, his historical novel about the American Revolution that would use the Maryland colony as a setting and John Paul Jones as a central figure.

By the end of the summer of 1897, this work was foremost in his mind. With Brett's acceptance of *The Celebrity* fresh in his mind, Churchill returned to the manuscript which he considered his first major effort. But the metropolitan area was never a place where he could do his best writing; there always seemed to be too many interruptions. Since St. Louis was where he had first craved history, in October of 1897 Churchill went west to St. Louis, where he rented an office in the Security Building, just down the hall from one occupied by Uncle James Gazzam.[2] In Room 503 Churchill set to work with the methodical ways of an office employee to finish his novel.

He had compiled a massive amount of notes, both from readings in history and fiction and from personal research into manuscript materials. At Annapolis the previous winter he had gone over court records, public documents, and old newspapers to learn something of the spirit of the old colony. He had interviewed people who could help in the re-creation of such an era. He had consistently approached the whole task with the thoroughness of a good researcher. "I prepared myself by visiting all the places concerned in the story, and by reading biographies, histories, memoirs, letters, old newspapers—in fact, everything which could give me an insight into the life of those days, or into the character of people like John Paul Jones and Charles Fox, whom I desired to introduce," he later told an interviewer.[3]

With earnestness and zeal, he worked at his first serious book. By late spring, 1898, he was still not satisfied with his manuscript, but he gave up the St. Louis office and returned to the East where he prepared to set to work once more. But now there were interruptions of another sort. The United States was about to make more history of its own, and Churchill could scarcely ignore it. On April 11, 1898, President McKinley succumbed to popular demand and asked Congress to declare war against Spain.

II

The Spanish-American War met with wide popular support. Some leading intellectuals and writers like Mark Twain, William Dean Howells, Carl Schurz, and Charles Francis Adams opposed the war, but many writers reflected public opinion by endorsing the venture. Churchill's favorable sentiments were presented in three mildly jingoistic writings published in the *Review of Reviews* and *Century* magazine during the summer of 1898.

The first of these journalistic pieces was a short biographical sketch of Admiral Dewey, America's new hero, written for the *Review of Reviews*.[4] The article is undistinguished but adequate journalism. Churchill briefly reviewed Dewey's life and then re-created the story of the Manila Bay engagement from the reports that had arrived. Dewey emerges as a great naval genius, the kind of portrait one might expect from a navy man and a strong contemporary patriot.

The second item occasioned by the Spanish-American War was a piece of fiction published in *Century* magazine in July, 1898. "By Order of the Admiral" was subtitled "A Story of the

Times," an indication that it was intended to appeal to the interest in the navy and naval affairs that the war produced. Churchill had started his writing career with this type of story; but "By Order of the Admiral" was his last decided attempt in that direction until he again turned to naval affairs during World War I.

In the story, Churchill tells how a young navy lieutenant meets the wealthy Victoria Knowlys at a New England coastal resort during the maneuvers of the North Atlantic Squadron. While the squadron is busy landing its "invading forces" against a defending unit of marines and while the society of the resort watches with curiosity, young Miss Knowlys displays her courage and audacity by riding her horse into the midst of the cannon fire. Even the admiral is impressed! He suggests to the young lady that such an enterprising woman should marry nothing less than a navy man and he suggests one of his own officers, Lieutenant Buckner.

In the days that follow, Buckner pursues the young lady as the admiral suggests, but he doesn't seem to be making much headway until he rescues her from a foolhardy attempt to sail her boat across the stormy bay of the coastal port. It is now her turn to be impressed with his courage and stamina. Weeks later, the young lady turns up again piloting her private yacht full of arms and munitions; she is smuggling weapons for the Cuban insurgents. Of course, she is overtaken by the admiral's squadron which is now patrolling the Atlantic Coast to prevent just such smuggling. Buckner is ordered to escort her, yacht and all, back to New York, and to make certain that she does not get away from him this time. Convinced that he is the man for her and encouraged by the admiral's written order, Victoria capitulates and agrees to marry the lieutenant just as the yacht sails into New York Harbor.

The story gets nowhere and the incidents are frequently ridiculous. Churchill displays his knowledge of how to sail ships and his acquaintance with the rules of naval strategy. But, more important, he also introduces the type of heroine that was to appeal to him in many of his future novels. Quite in keeping with the popularity of the type in other contemporary fiction, Churchill drew a portrait of a woman who loved the challenge of a struggle and who could command a filibuster as well as any man. Victoria Knowlys is a determined person with a decided mind of her own. She can tame a horse; she can manage a yacht; she knows military strategy and tactics. Indeed, by the admiral's own declaration, she is "a woman who would have done credit to a uniform, had she been a man."⁵ She loves to command: "All her life she had lived this creed with all her might."⁶ She will marry no namby-pamby, only a virile fellow who can match her, will for will. Buckner alone stands the test: "Never in all her life had any man put his will in direct opposition to her own without having to bend; but now this quiet young officer had spoken a few words, and his victory was complete. And, strangely enough, she rejoiced that it was so."⁷ Victoria is related to the super-woman who was to fight her way through the books of Jack London and Frank Norris in the literature of a strenuous age.

The third piece of journalism that Churchill wrote during the summer of 1898 was an account of the battle of Santiago Bay, published in *Review of Reviews* for August.⁸ Writing more in the vein of a professional historian than of a journalist, he gave an exciting account of the victory of July 3 that unquestionably thrilled his readers and added to their ever-growing pride in the United States fleet. Throughout, Churchill took pains to point out how the United States Navy had been underrated both in this country and abroad, and he did his best to add to the prestige of the navy and its importance in American defense. The eulogy of the navy and her commanders and crew was heightened with a certain feeling of Anglo-Saxon racial pride.

Churchill, of course, was swimming with the popular current when he urged the nation to greater concern with its fleet. Admiral Mahan had already written of the navy's importance, and Theodore Roosevelt was currently urging increased naval funds. The stress on the natural superiority of the Anglo-Saxon over the Latin races was also in keeping with contemporary interest. The Reverend Josiah Strong had been telling Americans ever since 1885, when his popular book *Our Country* was published, that the Anglo-Saxon was a superior type and that he would triumph in competition with other races, for numbers and wealth both favored him. Strong's doctrines were echoed for the next twenty years by the Progressives and expansionists who urged the Spanish-American War and the colonization of the Pacific—both popular ideas.

III

In October, 1898, the war with Spain ended. With no further thought of war service as a possible disruptive factor to his writing, Churchill continued with *Richard Carvel*, making efforts to get a final version ready for Macmillan. Always an indefatigable worker once he started on a novel and proposed to finish it, he rewrote *Richard Carvel* five times before he finally achieved the manuscript he wanted.

By April of 1899, he had completed the last version and delivered the manuscript to Brett. The publisher had been giving the novel considerable advance advertising, a technique of sales promotion that began to flourish in earnest in the 1890's. Contemporary newspaper accounts stated that the Macmillan Company spent over fifteen thousand dollars in ads for *Richard Carvel*. This was probably an exaggeration, but one reason for the tremendous sale the novel enjoyed was the heavy amount of propagandizing it had received before it ever appeared on the book stands. When Macmillan published *Richard Carvel* on June 1, 1899, it became an immediate best-seller.

Historical fiction was enjoying a great vogue at the time the novel appeared. The renewed burst of enthusiasm for cloak-and-dagger fiction about 1894 was caused at least partly by the influence of Robert Louis Stevenson whose work and personality had sparked the fires of romance in the late 1880's and early 1890's despite the increasing trend toward realism. For nearly a decade after Stevenson's death in 1894, the best-seller lists included historical romance of the old school, some of it serious work, most of it in the category of what Frank L. Mott has called "hammock thrillers."[9] Carl Van Doren suggests that the period between 1896 and 1902 produced "the most active school of historical romances" this country had ever seen.[10]

The Spanish-American War further enhanced the position of novels dealing with American history. The war itself had given Americans a growing sense of national self-consciousness; it had renewed the older feelings of manifest destiny and the newer ones of oceanic imperialism. Such a glorious, short flurry as the war with Spain produced—and the aftermath of overseas expansion in the Pacific—added zest to the American taste for patriotic, idealistic tracts. Though the historical novel might not directly celebrate America's new destiny, it provided the necessary, reassuring, idealistic background to justify the carrying of the flag to distant shores. The connection between glorification of the American past and the expansion of American principles was not hard to see.

Churchill did not write the novel deliberately to capture public taste; he was too serious in his own purposes to cater exclusively to popularity. *Richard Carvel* did appear, however, at precisely the right time to catch public fancy. It had idealism; it had a cloak-and-dagger plot; it had a number of popular historical figures, including George Washington; and it had plenty of Anglo-Saxon flag waving.[11] The novel was a contribution on the side of the romanticists in that struggle American fiction was going through in the 1890's. Churchill recalls the Victorian era, not the fiction of Crane or Norris or Dreiser. He is more like Bulwer-Lytton and Scott than like Howells. In the Boston *Herald* interview, Churchill said, "In writing of the 18th century one is almost compelled to treat the story romantically, because everybody has always done so, and to all intents and purposes, that is a romantic age."[12]

The story itself follows the closely knit pattern of a Thackeray novel. It relates the adventures that beset a young man who grows up in colonial Maryland, visits Georgian England, and returns to fight for the American cause in the Revolutionary War. Still a very readable adventure story, the best thing about the book is its atmosphere, its picture of the times, and the panorama of an era that it revives. The main characters move on and off the stage in puppet-like fashion; but there is a tone to the book that is authentic, and one reads it with the feeling that it is an accurate portrait of Maryland and England at the time of the Revolution.

The story is told in the first person by Richard Carvel, the protagonist of the novel. Like Churchill himself, Richard is an orphan. There are some mysteries about the parentage of Richard's mother, but Churchill makes it clear that this is not to be construed as casting any aspersions on the young hero's own station in life. Richard's grandfather cautions him to remember that he is a gentleman and is to seek no company "beyond that circle in which you were born."[13] This circle is manifestly that of upper-class Maryland society.

With both parents dead, Richard is reared by his grandfather, Lionel Carvel, a distinguished Maryland Tory who is sincere in his complete devotion to King George III. Through his associations in the town of Annapolis and through his early training at King William's School, Richard, on the other hand, has rapidly assumed rebel political notions. Since he holds his grandfather in the greatest affection and since he acknowledges his position under the guardianship of Grandfather Carvel, he holds his political views in check as much as a rather hot temper will allow.

Richard's troubles really start when a villainous uncle (one of the stock figures in such fiction) connives to cheat Richard of his lawful estate and has him kidnapped and carried to sea by pirates. The description of the ship, the *Black Moll*, and her crew seems patterned after Stevenson's *Treasure Island*. The pirates are overtaken in the Caribbean by a British ship commanded by Captain John Paul, later to be better known as John Paul Jones. In a swift engagement, the *Black Moll* is sunk, and Richard is rescued by Captain Paul's vessel, the brigantine *John* out of Kirkoudbright in Scotland.

The *John* is homeward bound for Scotland, and Richard is not too dismayed at the prospects of a voyage thence when he remembers that his sweetheart, Dorothy Manners, is now in England. John Paul becomes his close friend, and together they meet the hostility of the captain's own home folk when they reach Kirkoudbright. Goaded to a severe decision by the outspoken resentment of his countrymen at his strict discipline on his ships, John Paul takes permanent leave of his homeland and departs with Richard for London.

Carvel's experiences in London reflect the Georgian society of the day. After a time, his and John Paul's paths separate. Carvel finds his ladylove, but she is being courted by the wealthy Duke of Chartersea to whom her father is determined to marry her. Furthermore, her flirtations leave Richard somewhat nonplussed; he is never certain whether she loves him or not. Richard meets Lord Comyn, who duels with him first in a fine bit of swordplay and then becomes his close friend. The friendship with Comyn leads to close acquaintance with Charles James Fox. Fox is depicted in glowing terms as a dashing gay blade of a Whig who turns from an ardent king's man to a champion of the American cause. Other famous people introduced include Horace Walpole, Lord North, Lord Baltimore, David Garrick, Edmund Burke, and the Earl of Chatham. As Richard moves through this gaudy society, he visits the gaming-houses of White's, Almack's, and Brooks's, and he is introduced to the dissolute life of the king's set.

Adventures overtake him in rapid fashion. He is thrown into debtor's prison because his uncle's London agent turns out to be a rogue and refuses to advance him any funds. He incurs the enmity of his rival, the powerful Duke of Chartersea; he bests the duke in a test of horsemanship but is wounded later in a duel with him. He tests his political views on his London Tory friends, including the great Fox, and ends up admired by all—friend and foe alike—for his courage and forthrightness.

As political friction grows between the mother country and the colonies, Richard returns home to Annapolis. Since his grandfather has died in his absence, Uncle Grafton, his old enemy, has taken over "Carvel Hall." Richard is forced to seek residence elsewhere. His good patriot friend, Henry Swain, gives him opportunity to manage the plantation "Gordon's Pride." Richard proves his ability at management until the war comes; then he takes to the sea again, eventually ending up under the command of his old friend John Paul Jones, who is now fighting the colonists' cause against the homeland.

The war years are passed over rather fleetingly except for the account of the famous engagement between the *Bonhomme Richard* and the *Serapis*. Churchill had taken the name of his hero from one of the men who had served on the *Bonhomme Richard* with Jones. He wanted, above all else, to write an account of this naval battle, but his book was already too long. So he adopted the rather clumsy expedient of having Carvel's grandson Daniel Clapsaddle, the supposed editor of the book, give a résumé of the actions of Richard Carvel which culminated in the sea battle. The result is that the battle story seems dragged in as an afterthought, but the account of the engagement itself is well done. Churchill's knowledge of ships and naval affairs was put to good use here as elsewhere when he wrote of the sea.

After the *Serapis* battle, the story moves to a rapid conclusion. Richard, who has been wounded in the engagement, is taken to London to recuperate in the home of friends. The home turns out to be none other than that of his sweetheart, Dorothy Manners. Dorothy is now free to marry him; and, after his recuperation is complete, the two return to Annapolis to make their home. Wicked Uncle Grafton, who had switched loyalties during the war as circumstances warranted, was found out by the Maryland patriots. His illegal maneuvering, which had cheated Richard out of his grandfather's estate, was undone by legislative act, and Richard and Dorothy are able to return to the scene of much of their youthful happiness, "Carvel Hall."

The American reading public received Churchill's book as enthusiastically as it had taken to another Revolutionary War tale, Weir Mitchell's *Hugh Wynne*, the year before.[14] By the end of June, the book had gone through four printings, and was selling more than one thousand copies per day.[15] Later in the year and during the Christmas rush, orders for the book ran at twelve thousand a day.[16] Frank Luther Mott lists the book as a best-seller for 1899, meaning—according to his classification —that it sold at least 625,000 copies in the decade in which it was published.[17] Only E. N. Westcott's *David Harum* (1898) led *Richard Carvel* in the bookstores that summer, and *David Harum* faded from popularity in the next few years much sooner than Churchill's book. Macmillan had printed twelve editions by 1953, and three other publishers secured rights to print American editions in the two decades following the book's publication. The novel was translated into several languages in succeeding years, including German, French, and Italian. When one considers the American and foreign editions, it is clear that the book has sold well over a million copies.[18] It is apparent, too, that its popularity has lasted, for it is one of the few Churchill books still in print.

Furthermore, *Richard Carvel* not only captured the interest of the general public; it also received almost universal praise from the reviewers. Many American critics correctly saw its importance as an exact reproduction of an historical era. For this, the book was sometimes mentioned as "the great American novel" everyone had been seeking.[19]

Many English reviewers were also inclined to be kind. Interestingly, some of these reviewers and most of the English public were confusing the American Churchill and the English Churchill by this time. Many of the people who bought *Richard Carvel* in Britain thought that it was written by their own Winston S. Churchill, a situation that did nothing to hinder the sale of the book in England.

The most impressive aspect of *Richard Carvel* for a modern reader is its historical accuracy. Churchill spent the better part of four years preparing for and finishing the novel. As indicated earlier, he used contemporary newspaper reports of colonial Annapolis; he used interviews whenever they would be useful; he examined court records and legal documents of the colonial period. Furthermore, he consulted the most reliable secondary sources available at the time to get his picture of the era he was describing. Churchill acknowledged his debt to Thackeray, a stylistic influence most critics were quick to see, and pointed out that he had used Thackeray to get historical background for his novel. Boswell's *Life of Johnson* and Fielding served as models for his dialogue. Stevenson was another source, particularly for some of the sea drawings.

Churchill took his historical research conscientiously and made good use of it. "It is the business of historical fiction, as I conceive it, to give an absolutely faithful picture . . . of the thoughts, ideas, manners and customs, dress, occupations and pleasures of a given people in a given age," he told a Boston *Herald* interviewer.[20] The result of this careful rendering in *Richard Carvel* is the accurate "novel of manners" he attempted to write. It was the first fictional work to give any kind of portrayal of Annapolis society on the eve of the American Revolution. Prior to *Richard Carvel,* novelists had concentrated on the Northern colonies when dealing with the war for independence.

Churchill the historian was a decided success; but, when one turns to the artistic side of *Richard Carvel,* the faults of the popular fiction of that era seem painfully evident. To begin with, the use of the first-person narrative was unfortunate. The difficulty is that, as a hero of high romance, Carvel must be a dashing fellow, but he has to convey this impression by quoting what others have said about him. Since modesty is one of his attributes, he must remind the reader that these opinions are not necessarily his own. The autobiographical device therefore forces Richard to defend his modesty while displaying his exploits.

A more serious weakness of the novel is its poor character portrayal. With the exception of John Paul Jones, all the figures in *Richard Carvel* are like pasteboard models. They are vehicles Churchill uses to people a period. Richard Carvel soon becomes a bore; he can do nothing wrong. If he were just a little less sure on his horse, a little less at home upon the sea, and a little less dexterous with the sword, he might seem a little more of a real being and a little less Churchill's puppet. But in that case, he probably wouldn't have appealed to the women readers of 1899. Dorothy Manners, Richard's sweetheart, is a scintillating lady who can't quite make up her mind which man she wants to marry. She is a coquette, a popular type in the fiction of the time, but she moves too woodenly. She is a stereotyped beauty of gift-book genre. The villains (there are *three* of them) are right out of the worst melodrama. Only the old grandfather is convincing, and even he is a type rather than an individual.

The portrait of John Paul Jones is the exception, for it is the best fictional account of the naval hero up to that time. James Fenimore Cooper had dealt with him in *The Pilot,* but Churchill's Jones is a more human figure than Cooper's. Melville had used Jones in his *Israel Potter*; but most critics agree that Melville was at his poorest in this book. It would be foolish to argue that Churchill is in a class with Melville as a novelist; but, in his portrait of Jones and in his description of the *Serapis* defeat, he excels Melville in color, excitement, and authenticity. Reproducing the actual character of John Paul Jones with real thoroughness, Churchill depicts the great hero's supreme ability, his dauntless courage, and his moody eccentricities and inordinate vanity. Even the Scotch dialect has an authentic ring, if one can take the word of the English reviewers.[21]

Most readers of *Richard Carvel* saw the resemblance to Thackeray's *Henry Esmond* and *The Virginians*. Forty-two years before, Thackeray had created a hero of the colonies who visited London, knew "Horry" Walpole, played high, was in jail, and came home to fight with Washington. Richard Carvel is much like Harry Warrington of *The Virginians*. Uncle Grafton seems a little like Sir George Warrington, and Parson Allen is like Parson Sampson of the same book. Dorothy Manners is drawn after Beatrix Esmond of *Henry Esmond*. The whole scope of the book suggests *Vanity Fair* or *The Newcomes*. Thackeray's method of having a principal representative of a family chronicle its joys and sorrows was employed by Churchill in *Richard Carvel*.

But Churchill's attempt to weave as large an epic as Thackeray's resulted in a book that now seems far too long and laborious. The lack of plot originality becomes apparent before one has covered one-fourth of the five hundred pages which compose the. novel. Circumstance plays the all-important role. Heroes are always right, and villains are always dark and vicious. In truth, the very things that appealed to the reading public (especially the female reader) in 1899 make the action seem crude today. Such fiction always had to have a good fight, particularly of the swordplay variety. Churchill made good use of his fencing instruction at Annapolis to include enough duels to catch the reader's fancy. Horses and horse racing were popular elements in the fiction of the age, and Churchill put in just enough to make the ladies gasp and admire. And there is the sweet, willful, impossibly beautiful woman whom the black villains pursue and whom the hero weds on the next to last page. Above all, virtue is always rewarded; vice meets its deserts. Such contrivances tend to annoy or amuse the sophisticated modern reader, but they clearly represent the taste of 1899.

Charles Walcutt has accurately called *Richard Carvel* "episodic."[22] Yet, this is what Churchill tried to avoid. He said that he did not create a skeleton of the whole book, chapter by chapter, and then simply write it according to plan. "You can do that in the episodical novel, which consists merely of a chain of adventures, one following another from beginning to end. But when you are writing a novel of manners and customs it is different. I drew up a long summary of *Richard Carvel* and referred to it and changed it constantly."[23] Churchill persistently referred to *Carvel* as a novel of manners and customs. This it is; but it is also a novel of episodes. Insofar as he created fiction, the story is simply a chronological listing of the adventures the hero passes through. As an episodic novel, the book fails. But as a novel of manners and customs, it succeeds; in this respect, what Churchill attempted, he achieved.

The enormous success of *Richard Carvel* brought Churchill financial independence and personal fame. He soon became the

subject of newspaper stories and the object of magazine inter-
viewers whenever they could get to him. His comings and goings
became worthy of news comment; his opinions on literary matters
were sought after. The name "Richard Carvel" itself became so
famous that companies began to bring out products bearing the
appellation. People from all over the world began writing him
letters, and he was generally lionized wherever he went.

But perhaps the greatest proof of Churchill's new fame
came when, in the summer of 1899, he received a communication
from an English Churchill suggesting that too much mistaken
identity was resulting because two writers were named Winston
Churchill. The Englishman added that he had decided hence-
forth to sign his books and papers "Winston Spencer Churchill"
to avoid confusion with the American. Since he had no middle
name, the American was glad to acknowledge this courtesy on
the part of the other author. He noted that he intended to ask
his publishers about the advisability of inserting the words
"The American" on his own title pages. Nothing ever came of
this suggestion, however; and for several years more mistakes
were made, particularly in England, by reviewers and the reading public. In the United States, the American was soon far
better known than the Englishman.[24]

IV

In 1899, the Churchills moved to Cornish, New Hampshire,
where they had been drawn by the beauty of the countryside.
Cornish was a "town" in the New England sense; there was
little commercial settlement, not even a post office, in the community. But it was the home of a number of writers and artists,
including Augustus Saint-Gaudens, perhaps America's greatest
sculptor; Kenyon Cox, the "genre" painter; Stephen and Maxfield
Parrish; Herbert Croly; Robert Herrick (for a brief time);
Norman Hapgood; and Percy MacKaye. Louis Shipman, the
playwright, had a home there; Charles A. Platt, the architect,
was a Churchill neighbor. In addition, prominent wealthy
businessmen and lawyers from New York had summer residences
in the area. The Cornish community even then had a minor
reputation in the East as a center for artists and intellectuals.

Here in the New Hampshire hills, on a bluff overlooking the Connecticut River valley, the Churchills had built "Harlakenden House," their permanent home. An interviewer for *National Magazine,* Joe Mitchell Chapple, who came to visit the author in his new quarters in the fall of 1899, reported that the house "had a stately Carvel dignity about it." As he toured the grounds and strolled with Churchill through the interior, he was reminded of Scott's "Abbotsford" and the outlook upon the Tweed. All in all, he felt there was "a feeling of appropriateness that the author of 'Richard Carvel' should dwell therein."[25]

Apparently Churchill now had the surroundings he felt he needed for his work. He was not averse to wealth and what it could bring, but he also had a higher purpose for his writing. "In Richard Carvel I have laid the foundation for a series of novels that will deal with several of the most emphasized epochs in the history of this country," he said.[26] As Pattee puts it, "Like Roosevelt he too would write the saga of America, the romance of the winning of the western world."[27] Before *Richard Carvel* was published, Churchill knew what his next book would be. He already had considerable material on the Civil War days in St. Louis, and there were people in his home city who could give him much more firsthand data for a good Civil War story. Such a work began to fit into his new plan of becoming one of the historical novelists for the nation.

Specifically, he conceived the notion of writing five historical books covering the growth and progress of the United States from the colonial period through the Civil War and Reconstruction and presenting the material from the Anglo-Saxon viewpoint. He did not contemplate bringing the series down through the period of the war with Spain, for he felt that historical novels could be written only thirty or forty years after the period which they described. The over-all purpose of his writing would be to teach history as much as to amuse the readers. Several years later, after Churchill had abandoned historical fiction, critics were fond of remarking that he had turned to the problem novel. But as early as 1899 Churchill seems to have thought of his books as serving to educate American readers. He also felt the novel could heighten their interest in government and educate them about the privileges and responsibilities they enjoyed as members of the Anglo-Saxon community.

Churchill decided not to write his series in chronological order, and in the summer of 1899 he started work on his Civil War novel, *The Crisis*. Working with the methodicalness which grew from his feeling that writing was "a direct means to a direct end,"[28] Churchill read his sources and compiled his notes into the fall. In December, he decided to return to St. Louis to get further materials for the story. Again he temporarily established his office in the Security Building, the same place where he had composed so much of *Richard Carvel*.

The St. Louis visit proved profitable. Churchill went about seeking the testimony of all those who would cooperate in providing authentic material for the book. James E. Yeatman, one of St. Louis' foremost philanthropists and a Southerner by birth, gave him manuscripts and reminiscences about the war. Yeatman, beloved by both rebels and unionists, had been in charge of the Western Sanitary Commission in St. Louis in 1864 and 1865. Isaac Sturgeon, Comptroller of the city in 1899, but Assistant United States Treasurer in St. Louis in 1861, had been a Union man and had spent the greater part of the war in Missouri. Judge Leo Rassieur, later a commander of the Grand Army of the Republic; Charles Nagel, a prominent lawyer; and, above all, Henry Hitchcock, another leading lawyer and a friend, gave him valuable data. Many of Mrs. Churchill's relatives and friends were from old families in the city, and Churchill made full use of these associations. Indeed, he unquestionably had some of these people in the back of his mind when he drew his characters for the book; in fact, some St. Louis readers later called *The Crisis* the story of Churchill's wife's relatives.

But Churchill did not rely exclusively on personal contacts. He made great use of Sherman's and Grant's memoirs—for both of these notables were to appear in the novel—and he read the new histories by James Ford Rhodes as they came out. Lives of Grant and Lincoln further extended his knowledge of the period.

The Crisis was finally published in May, 1901, after Churchill had done considerable revision as usual. His second venture into the historical field, this novel was also his most successful and most lasting attempt and is the one most often recalled by Churchill admirers.

Like *Richard Carvel*, *The Crisis* is a romance with a personal story that has serious shortcomings but with a large historical canvas that is both accurate and well drawn. It depicts the conflict between the North and the South during the Civil War, particularly as it developed in the border city of St. Louis. Churchill explained that he had chosen St. Louis as the setting for most of the story because of the co-mingling of the two westward tides of migration in that region. "Puritan and Cavalier united on this clay-bank in the Louisiana Purchase, and swept westward together. Like the struggle of two great rivers when they meet, the waters for a while were dangerous."[29] In addition, Churchill wanted to tell the story of the Germans in St. Louis during the Civil War era. Their story had never been adequately told, and Churchill thought it was an important and interesting segment of American history worth recounting. Most of all, of course, he knew St. Louis and its people. He was writing from a firsthand acquaintance with some of the actual participants in the events he related.

The Crisis bears somewhat the same relationship to *Richard Carvel* that Thackeray's *Virginians* bears to *Henry Esmond*. The hero of *The Virginians* was the descendent of Henry Esmond; so Virginia Carvel in *The Crisis* is the great-granddaughter of Richard Carvel, while Colonel Comyn Carvel, the aristocratic Southerner who resembles Thackeray's Colonel Newcome, is the grandson of Richard. Churchill probably adopted this fictional device from his avowed master in the historical novel.

Writing in the third person, the author tells the story of Stephen Brice who had left Boston after the death of his prominent lawyer-father to journey to St. Louis in 1856 to practice law in the office of his father's friend, Judge Whipple. Though Judge Whipple is a Republican and an Abolitionist, he manages to keep up a close friendship with Colonel Carvel, the head of a great wholesale dry goods store and a typical southern Democrat. Through Judge Whipple, Stephen makes the acquaintance of Virginia Carvel, daughter of the colonel. Stephen and Virginia are immediately drawn to each other by a magnetic, romantic attachment that neither understands. Virginia fights this attraction, however, because of Stephen's Northern sympathies and becomes engaged to a romantic cavalier Southerner named Clarence Colfax.

When war breaks out, Stephen and Virginia are on opposite sides of the conflict. Virginia must be true to her Southern birth and principles; her father is an ardent Southerner; and her fiancé is one of the first to enlist in the Confederate cause. Stephen, on the other hand, has been thoroughly revolted by a slave auction he saw shortly after his arrival in St. Louis; he has been schooled in Republican doctrines by Judge Whipple; and he has seen and met a young lawyer named Abraham Lincoln during the famous debate with Judge Douglas at Free-port, Illinois. He can scarcely help supporting the Union cause.

Stephen finally enlists in the Union army, though he hesitates at first because he is the sole support of his mother. He serves under Sherman, whom he comes to idolize and call "my general"; meets General Grant; and eventually becomes an aide to President Lincoln by the end of the war. At one point during the struggle, he is brought home wounded. He is nursed back to health by his mother and by Virginia, who, despite her political leanings, admits a strong emotional attachment to Stephen. Clarence Colfax, Virginia's betrothed, fights valiantly with the Confederates. But despite his dashing, romantic ways, Virginia confesses at last that she does not really love him.

As the war is ending, the two lovers meet in Washington and are manipulated into the presence of Abraham Lincoln. Virginia —who is completely captivated by the generosity, the kindness, and especially the sorrow of Lincoln—has come to plead for the life of Clarence Colfax, captured as a spy by Sherman's army. She learns that Stephen has already interceded for Colfax, and that Lincoln will pardon the young Southerner. Virginia, who breaks under such kindness, wishes that everyone in the South might see Lincoln as she has seen him so that Southern bitter-ness might be eliminated. In the next to last chapter the two lovers are reconciled to symbolize the new unity of North and South that Lincoln sought. The last scene finds them in Annapolis roaming through the haunts of Richard Carvel, Virginia's an-cestor, and speculating on the "force" that brought them together.

Against the background of this rather melodramatic love story, Churchill draws in some interesting side issues. One of the more important concerns the large German element of St. Louis. One of Brice's close friends is Karl Richter, a university-bred revolutionist who has fled Germany in the upheavals of 1848 and has come to St. Louis. There he is representative of the German population that did so much to save the city and Missouri for the Union cause in 1861.

Churchill's villain is an unpleasant Northerner who is without principle or pity. Driven by greed and ambition, Eliphalet Hopper seeks only profit from the war; it matters not to him which side wins so long as he makes his money. He drives Colonel Carvel to economic ruin in his dry goods business and attempts to arrange a marriage with Virginia. Through the noble intercessions of Stephen Brice, Virginia is saved from such an undesirable fate.

Represented also is the Southerner who fights with the Union. Captain Elisha Brent of Mississippi River steamboat fame is a good friend of Colonel Carvel. He is a pro-slavery man but will have no part in breaking up the nation. Reluctantly, he is forced into the position of opposing the colonel and the South.[30]

Through the novel roam the historic figures of Sherman, Grant, Lincoln, Frémont, Francis Blair, and Nathaniel Lyon. For the most part, they are shown before their rise to greatness (except for Frémont), always as plain people of the West who stepped forth onto the stage of history at just the right time to save the Union. Characteristically, Churchill does a better job in picturing them than he does with his fictional figures.

It soon became apparent that Churchill had caught popular fancy even more effectively with *The Crisis* than he had with *Richard Carvel*. The first edition of one hundred thousand copies was sold out six days after publication, and eventually the novel went through more than fourteen editions for the American Macmillan alone. There were also American editions by Grosset and Dunlap; in addition, there were numerous foreign editions. The book remains Churchill's best-selling, best-known work.[31]

Oddly, in view of its immense popularity, *The Crisis* met a more mixed reaction with the critics than *Richard Carvel*. It had a considerable share of enthusiastic reviews; Richard Henry Stoddard, Hamilton Mabie, and Richard Watson Gilder were among those lavish in their praise. But there were dissenters, not only among Southerners who thought Churchill was pro-Union and among Northerners who thought he was pro-South, but among those critics who now voiced objections to Churchill's literary art. Both William Dean Howells and Frank Norris, who expressed their annoyance at the sales such romantic books could command, found little to praise in either *Richard Carvel* or *The Crisis*. Julian Hawthorne, son of Nathaniel, wrote one of the most scathing reviews that Churchill ever received; he called him only a poor imitator of Thackeray and Charles Reade who "has the misfortune to touch nothing that he does not vulgarize and confuse."[32] These were minority voices, but they expressed the consensus of a small group of reviewers and critics who seemed to feel that Churchill was an overrated author.

Political figures, however, such as Vice-President Theodore Roosevelt and Senator Albert Beveridge found the book exciting because of the good lesson it gave in American history. No doubt many of the readers of the early 1900's liked it for precisely the same reasons. Churchill depicts well the St. Louis of the 1850's and the early 1860's—the bustling river wharves, the slave market, the ante-bellum Southern homes, the more recent Northern immigration, and the German colony. The historical figures who move in this setting are impressive and accurate. Ernest E. Leisy has said that *The Crisis* has "the best portrayal of Abraham Lincoln in a novel of the Civil War"[33]; and Major Hoyt Sherman, brother of the famous general, is said to have reported that the portrait of his brother was accurate and completely in keeping with his character. Grant seems authentic, even to a modern reader. The historical scenes are all drawn with precision and with color. All in all, Churchill's reliance on historical accuracy is, if anything, even more impressive in *The Crisis* than in *Richard Carvel*. Still eminently readable because of its history, *The Crisis* is probably the only fictional account that gives the full and true story of the part the German element played in keeping Missouri in the Union. And it was one of the first Civil War novels written from a Western point of view. This probably accounted for its general acceptance in both the North and the South.

Agnes Repplier had written, "He takes admirable care of his history, and leaves his fiction to look after itself."[34] Readers in the early 1900's, however, liked the book for its romantic plot. The Boston *Herald* reported in October of 1902 on the ingredients of the popular novel: "It must have sentiment; the sweetheart must keep her lover at arm's length; the hero must not win her too easily; the sweetheart must alternately draw him on and baffle him, fire and freeze him; she must have some ginger, some 'get-up-and-go'; the hero must be handsome, a woman's man, with something of the patrician in his look; the heroine must be altogether patrician in birth, manner, and bearing; there must be a villain who meets a picturesque, dire fate; above all, no new ideas about the country or the people may be introduced."[35] Certainly *The Crisis* meets all the standards set forth by this article; there is abundant sentiment, and the hero and heroine move in situations governed largely by happy chance. Though the plot is more coherent than that of *Richard Carvel*, it is still manipulated to suit the needs of the historical panorama. Churchill would use any story, one suspects, provided it fitted into the larger canvas he was painting.

Most of the fictional characters move even more woodenly than in *Richard Carvel*. Stephen Brice, though patterned after a living man, Henry Hitchcock, is only the stock character of romantic melodrama. He is a paragon of all virtue, a blue-blood, and more of a prig than Richard Carvel. Virginia Carvel is nothing more than the combined portrait of several girls of Southern lineage whom Churchill knew in St. Louis. She is not an individual, but the traditional type of ante-bellum spitfire. Colonel Comyn Carvel is the shopworn Southern colonel, complete with goatee, who speaks with a drawl, and yells "whoopee" and says "I reckon" and "suh" at every turn. Eliphalet Hopper seems reminiscent of Uriah Heep. If ever there was a darker villain, melodrama never displayed him. Judge Whipple is a lifeless type who serves as the mouthpiece for the Republican party and abolitionist sentiment. Clarence Colfax is the usual dashing, hot-headed Southerner, gallant and impetuous, with more courage than judgment. Stereotypes they all are—examples of viewpoints that Churchill used for illustrative purposes. The one exception (there always seems to be one exception in a Churchill novel) is Calvin Brinsmade, the only character that Churchill freely admitted he drew from life. His model was James E. Yeatman, the man to whom he had dedicated *Richard Carvel*. Brinsmade is an effective fictional portrait. Torn between two devotions as the great crisis approaches and explodes, loyal to the Union but sympathetic to the South, he is the one character in the book who is acceptable to both sides in the struggle;

and he is the one character who possesses sufficient individuality to come alive.

The style of the book is undistinguished, and it is further marred by occasional annoying lapses in syntax. Observing a slave auction, Stephen Brice thinks, "But his father, nor his father's friends, had never been brought face to face with this hideous traffic."[36] At another point in the book, "Virginia hid her face in her handkerchief, which trembled visibly. Being a woman, whose ways are unaccountable, the older man took no notice of her. But being a young woman, and a pretty one, Stephen was angry."[37] The reviewer in *Bookman* magazine must have had such passages in mind when he wrote that "*The Crisis* is without the slightest touch of genius."[38]

No city was more enthusiastic in its reception of *The Crisis* than St. Louis. The novel brought new fame to the places the author had depicted: the court house; the ancient mansion of "Bellegarde"; Glencoe, twenty-five miles to the southeast; the streets and scenes of his youth. The St. Louis *Post-Dispatch* reported in 1903 that "there is much interest on the part of tourists to St. Louis to see the scenes of *The Crisis*."[39] A successful stage version of the play brought added fame to author and city, and many who earlier had only read of Stephen Brice and Virginia Carvel later saw their story acted out by two leading road companies of the day.

V

The Crisis further insured Churchill's financial security and his public acclaim. A New York *Times* correspondent reported in 1901, "To all intents and purposes Mr. Churchill's existence is that of the majority of the members of the landed gentry of Britain—horses, dogs, hunting, tennis, books, and friends—these fill out the hours of the day in most delightful manner."[40] He was proud to drive his four-in-hand coach around Cornish, and he and Mrs. Churchill were known as two of the foremost horse enthusiasts in the area. There were occasional jaunts to the seashore and fishing trips in Canada. In between came long hours at his work desk, though he was taking some time off to test his talents in a new direction—oratory.

In the summer of 1901, Churchill accepted an invitation to speak at the dedication of the Louisiana Purchase Building at the Pan-American Exposition in Buffalo, New York. His first major speaking engagement, it was almost as great a success as his first major novel.

Furthermore, the Exposition speech boded well for another interest that was soon to attract his attention and demand his energies—politics. Late in that summer of 1901 Churchill made the acquaintance of the Vice-President of the United States, Theodore Roosevelt. Churchill was quickly captured by the magnetism of Roosevelt's personality, and the future President was always eager to encourage a writer of the romantic school. By the autumn of that year, Churchill was attending dinners at the White House and was being drawn toward the progressivism of the new President.

Meanwhile, Churchill was tentatively planning his next historical novel; it would deal with the period in United States history immediately following the Revolution, the first westward movement. After a six-month tour of Europe, during which he met and talked with the Kaiser in Germany and the English Churchill in London, he returned to St. Louis to begin his story. It was to occupy him for the better part of three years. *The Crossing*, the third volume in the historical series, was published in May, 1904, in time to coincide with the St. Louis World's Fair-Exposition celebrating the Louisiana Purchase.[41]

Churchill had first contemplated writing a novel of the period from the first westward crossings through the coming of the steamboat to the Mississippi Valley, but it proved too formidable a task. He decided to reserve the War of 1812 and the steamboat era for another story—a story, as it turned out, that was never written. Churchill admitted that he had "a great sense of [*The Crossing's*] incompleteness."[42] One of its faults is its diffuseness, its lack of cohesion. Any one of the areas Churchill was attempting to deal with would have been adequate material for a historical romance. As it is, there are too many scenes, and they are crowded together in too rapid a sequence.

The novel is largely the autobiography of David Ritchie, "born under the Blue Ridge" in the western part of North Carolina. Like Richard Carvel and like Churchill himself, young Davy grows up without the care of his mother, for she has died in his infancy. In Book I, "The Borderland," the author tells how Davy's father goes off to fight the Cherokees after leaving his son with his sister-in-law, Mrs. Temple, in the tidewater town of Charlestown. The father is killed in the ensuing Indian war (actually a part of the American Revolution), and young Davy is left to the care of his aunt who has neither time nor love for him. Mrs. Temple is too busy carrying on an illicit love affair with Harry Riddle to be very much concerned with her own son, Nick, or with her young nephew. Were it not for the new friendship with his boisterous young cousin, Nick Temple, Davy's lot would be unbearable indeed.

As it is, when news comes of the death of his father, the lad can stand the life at "Temple Bow" no longer. He flees one night and heads back toward the mountains. He eventually meets Polly Ann Ripley and her father who are also on their way to the Blue Ridge country. Davy accompanies them to their mountain home. When, shortly after their arrival, Polly Ann marries her pioneering lover, Tom McChesney, young Davy goes with them as they cross into Tennessee, through Cumberland Gap, and over the Wilderness Trail to a new home in Kentucky. Some of Churchill's best writing comes in describing this overland trek. One chapter, "On the Wilderness Trail," is as good a description of a pioneer journey as one can find in fiction.

At their destination, Harrodstown, the pioneers learn of the Indian troubles originating to the north. The American Revolution is in progress, and the British are stirring up the tribes to murder and pillage the outlying frontiers. A natural pioneer leader and scout named George Rogers Clark has the answer to this: he proposes an expedition across the Ohio into the Indian country to destroy the British forts located there. Subsidized by the Virginia government, Clark leads a plucky little band of backwoodsmen into the Illinois country in 1778 to wrest the territory from the enemy. David Ritchie goes along as the little drummer boy actually mentioned by Clark in his memoirs. The youth's courage and determination are a constant inspiration to the hard-pressed little band as they push through the woods and swamps to Kaskaskia, Cahokia, and finally to Vincennes. The story of the Clark expedition had already been told fictionally by Maurice Thompson in *Alice of Old Vincennes* (1900), but Churchill does a better job than Thompson in bringing out the epic quality of Clark's march through the Wabash country and in pointing to the significance of Clark's expedition in deciding the fate of the North American continent. If he is guilty of overdrawing Clark's contribution to the westward movement, he can be excused on the grounds that practically all the historians of this era gave it the same importance. Book I ends with the fall of Vincennes and with the return of Davy and his friend Tom McChesney to their home in Harrodstown, Kentucky.

Churchill should have ended his book at this point, for he had written some of his best history. "The Borderland" remains a stirring account of the early Tennessee-Kentucky settlements and a noteworthy fictional portrayal of the Clark expedition. As a boy's book, the account is perhaps unsurpassed in juvenile fiction dealing with the Wilderness Road and George Rogers Clark.

But Churchill chose to extend his story beyond the Revolution. He had done considerable research on the James Wilkinson-Spanish plot against the new federal government and he wished to include this subject in his fictional treatment. So in the novel the years pass rapidly. The reader learns of the new troubles over land policies in the trans-Appalachian area. Trade matters and the situation at New Orleans are bothering the Kentuckians. Even Daniel Boone is muttering against the national government. Davy goes off to Virginia to study law and shortly matures into as fine a Federalist protégé as old Judge Wentworth, his tutor, can make him. He journeys back over the mountains to visit the new state of Franklin in the Tennessee country and to find leaders in Kentucky intriguing with the Spanish minister Miro to secede from the new nation and join the King of Spain. John Sevier, Andrew Jackson, and Colonel John Tipton are introduced in rapid sequence.

Shortly, Davy again meets his old hero, George Rogers Clark, now an embittered old man, neglected by the nation he had served so well. "The treatment he has had would bring a blush of shame to the cheek of any nation save a republic. Republics are wasteful, sir. In George Rogers Clark they have thrown away a general who might some day have decided the fate of this country, they have left to stagnate a man fit to lead a nation to war. And now he is ready to intrigue against the government with any adventurer who may have convincing ways and a smooth tongue."[43] James Wilkinson is the adventurer who meets the description; he has talked Clark into joining his grandiose schemes, albeit Davy and a Federalist friend, Mr. Wharton, can only make good guesses and surmises as to what they involve.

Mr. Wharton sends Davy on an expedition first to St. Louis and then to New Orleans to see what he can discover about the Wilkinson-Miro plot. After one excellent chapter telling about the trip down the Mississippi—"The Keel Boat," a chapter reminiscent of Mark Twain's *Life on the Mississippi*—Churchill slips into some of the worst writing he ever did. He gradually leaves the historical scenes and creates sentimental fiction. Davy has run across his childhood friend and cousin, Nick Temple, again. Nick accompanies him to New Orleans and almost takes over the story when the two meet Phillipe de St. Gré and his beautiful daughter Antoinette. Davy is left by the way as impetuous Nick pursues Antoinette. The pursuit is interrupted long enough for Nick to damn his mother, Mrs. Temple, who is found living in seclusion at the home of the St. Gré's, a pitiful remnant of her former proud self, and deserted by her lover Harry Riddle. Nick gets mixed up in the Wilkinson business, and Davy is hard pressed to keep his friend from making a fool of himself.

Some few years later, Davy makes another trip to New Orleans, again unofficially in the interests of his country. With complete Federalist sympathies and with French Loyalist proclivities, he meets Hélène d'Ivry-le-Tour, a widowed exile from Revolutionary France and a member of the old Royalist order. She is one who has known Marie Antoinette, and Churchill's apparent fascination with aristocratic societies is revealed when he has Hélène tell of the grand days at the French court and of the high society that has been destroyed by the damnable Jacobins. Hélène is a bit old for Davy, and, judging by her portrait reproduced in the first edition of the book, she is no beauty. But Davy finds her enchanting and a match for any man. He finally wins her to American Federalist ways, after she has nursed him through a yellow fever siege that sweeps New Orleans. With her Loyalist sentiments reconciled to the New World ("You are all kings in America, are you not?"[44]), Hélène consents to return with Davy to his Kentucky home where he will resume the practice of law in Louisville.

Churchill is hazy about the precise nature of Davy's visits to

New Orleans, but one can assume he successfully accomplished his missions, whatever their purposes may have been. The book ends with the transfer several years later of the Louisiana Territory to the United States. Davy, as he contemplates the destiny that has set in motion the growth of the new nation, looks to the future with hope and a touch of foreboding: "What had God in store for the vast land out of which the waters flowed? Had He, indeed, saved it for a People, a People to be drawn from all nations, from all classes? Was the principle of the Republic to prevail and spread and change the complexion of the world? Or were the lusts of greed and power to increase until in the end they had swallowed the leaven? Who could say? What man of those who, soberly, had put his hand to the Paper which declared the opportunities of generations to come, could measure the Force which he had helped to set in motion?"[45] As early as 1904, Churchill's Progressive reform tendencies were beginning to appear. He was to write no more historical fiction; the ending of *The Crossing* seems already to point in another direction.

Fred Lewis Pattee reports that, upon the publication of *The Crossing* in 1904, Churchill "awoke to find himself all but alone. Overnight historical romance had become a commodity outmoded and unsalable. No one was reading it. The era of 'the strenuous life' was on."[46] This was largely true; Churchill himself by 1904 was increasingly involved in political reform. But it would be incorrect to call *The Crossing* "unsalable," or to say that "no one was reading it." The book was a best-seller for two years after its publication, and numerous editions during the next twenty years attested to its popularity with the American and European reading public. It seems safe to say that the book has sold well over five hundred thousand copies in all its editions—not a bad total for a romance published in the twilight if not the evenfall of the great historical fad of the turn of the century.

The friendly treatment that Churchill had received from the reviewers with his first books was considerably tempered when it came to *The Crossing*. Many critics were now apologizing for his literary qualities, though they consistently found that he had won new laurels as an historian. Numerous reviewers remarked on the great care with which Churchill always constructed his novels, but there was a tendency to take a second look at his narrative skill. He was, these critics said, an accomplished work-man, but not a finished literary artist. Some were suggesting, too, that Churchill had an uncanny sense of measuring public demand in fiction—that he wrote his novels to meet some new public interest. (*The Crossing* was published at the exact time George Rogers Clark Day was being celebrated at the Louisiana Purchase Exposition in St. Louis.) Such reviewers were ap-parently unaware of Churchill's high moral concern and earnest-ness of purpose—certainly there was no calculated intent on his part to capture fads of the moment.

The Crossing has many of the faults of its predecessors. There is a failure to create real, human characters. In Book I, David Ritchie is a child prodigy with all the wisdom of a Solomon, the craft of a Ulysses, and the physical dexterity of a Daniel Boone. As the writer in the *Critic* put it, "He is an all-wise, all-efficient midget of eleven years, drummer-boy, coun-selor, and prophet."[47] In short, Davy is beyond reality. And he does not improve much with age; he becomes the typical protag-onist of popular romantic literature. The other characters move just as mechanically through their roles as Ritchie does. Nick Temple almost takes on life, but Churchill spoils it all by making him a foil for Davy's sobriety later in the novel. The backwoods figures seem a little more lifelike, but they are all reflections of what Churchill had read about Daniel Boone. George Rogers Clark is the best of the historical figures, although Churchill idealizes him; the result is a paragon of patriotic leadership and virtue who can do no wrong. Actually, history says some-thing different.

Book I is an exciting odyssey of Davy's journey across the mountains, but Books II and III elaborate a sprawling plot that becomes clumsy before the end is reached. In addition, the fictional action degenerates into as high melodrama as one finds anywhere. There are no surprises; one knows all the answers before they are reached. The humor seldom makes one laugh; the pathos fails to move a modern reader, though it may have had its effect in 1904. The novel is spoiled by the extended trappings of the sentimental love element in the latter two-thirds.

What moves today's reader is not the individuals in the book but the historical events and the scenes of the westward epoch as

Churchill unfolds them. A. E. Hancock accurately stated, "In matters of detail, he falls behind his own contemporaries. But in the reach and grasp of panoramic effects, vibrant with the march of national evolution, and charged with the electric energy that resists and overcomes, he is easily the chief. To put it in another way, his strength lies not in the clear-cut figures of the foreground, but in the immense suggestiveness of the background."[48] As in his other historical romances, one is impressed by the epic effect, the comprehensive picture. The following historical scenes are good: the British attack on Charleston; the fight with the Indians on the Wilderness Road; the descent on Kaskaskia; the march through the wilderness to Vincennes; the capture of Hamilton, the British commander; the passage down the Mississippi in a flatboat; the picture of Creole New Orleans. These descriptions have the color and the ring of the genuine. When Churchill was telling again the old stories of America's past, he was at his best. He could render the spirit of a time with a fine, sympathetic accuracy. When he moved into the more imaginative realms of fictional creation, he faltered.

Many of the contemporary reviewers, recognizing this characteristic by 1904, were saying that Churchill was primarily an historian, not a fiction writer. Herbert Croly, in discussing Edith Wharton, Gertrude Atherton, and Churchill as historical novelists, said that "when they write historical novels, the stories they tell, if they tell any at all, are subordinated to an attempt at historical or biographical representation."[49] Senator Albert Beveridge, who could vouch for historical worth with some authority, was always impressed by Churchill's capacity to recall bygone eras and the spirit of a time in his fiction.[50] The historians themselves lauded the author's qualities. Professors Albert Bushnell Hart of Harvard and James Ford Rhodes were among those who acclaimed Churchill's historical novels. Indeed, as late as 1949, another leading historian, Henry Steele Commager of Columbia University, recommended *The Crossing* for the accuracy with which it was written.[51]

As historian, then, Churchill's reputation was high in his own day, and it has remained so as the years have passed. He can be given credit—and it is no small accolade—for adding something to the historical romance that was lacking before, namely, accurate, painstaking research. Unlike his predecessors and his contemporaries who wrote such fiction, he was a chronicler whose meticulosity was worthy of the best historian's craft. One could wish that Churchill had turned his wonderful story-telling talents to the fields of pure history or biography. He would then have been a literary historian—perhaps in the tradition of Parkman, Prescott, or Motley. As it is, he left three popular examples of the romancer's craft which are mediocre as fictional art though still highly readable today. If one must take his early American history with a fictionalized coating, there is no better place to get it than in these three novels that gave Winston Churchill his early fame and fortune.

CHAPTER 3

Politics and the Political Novels

I

HISTORICAL ROMANCE, so popular in the 1890's, quickly lost favor with the coming of the twentieth century. *The Crossing* had appeared just at the end of a popular reading fad. Successful though it was, it still did not match the sales of *Richard Carvel* or *The Crisis*. Different interests were occupying the public mind and Churchill himself was very soon caught up in the new enthusiasms.

The muckrakers were awakening the reading public to the lure of the exposé and to the need for reform. The propaganda novel revealing graft, corruption, and private greed became the new best-seller. Lisle Abbott Rose, in a survey of political and economic fiction published between 1902 and 1909, lists thirty-six such novels issued in 1902, forty-seven in 1903, one hundred and five in 1905-6, forty in 1908, and twenty in the first six months of 1909. Rose lists a total of 331 titles for the seven-year period. More significantly, the peak in popularity for such novels occurred between September, 1905, and March, 1907. After a slight fall-off in interest, there was a renewal from May, 1908, to June, 1909.[1] With *Coniston* in June, 1906, and with *Mr. Crewe's Career* in May, 1908, Churchill made his contribution to these political publications.

The author, of course, had compelling reasons by this time for writing political novels. He had gained experience in the rough-and-tumble of state-house politics. Churchill's own sense of duty as an American citizen had propelled him into the Progressive crusades that were to dominate the next twelve years of American party politics. The initial impulse for Churchill's interest in politics probably came from Theodore Roosevelt, although the times in 1902 were propitious for the author to attempt the practice of some of his reform theories. At any rate, Churchill made the plunge into local politics soon after he had met the young President he was to admire so much over the next decade.

Fred L. Pattee has said, "The spirit of the President influenced the decade like a fortissimo *motif*. . . . From 1901 to the end of the decade is the era of Theodore Roosevelt. He dominated the whole decade like a major chord."[2] Above all, Roosevelt dominated the intellectual currents of "The Strenuous Age." His biographer, Henry F. Pringle, says that "he was far more of a scholar, despite the prejudices which clouded his historical writings, than most of the men who had been in the White House."[3] For the first time in at least four decades, a literary and intellectual man was President. Many writers of the moment were caught up in his orbit, for Roosevelt considered himself something of a critic. Generally opposed to realism and bitterly antagonistic to Zola and naturalism, he did his best to bolster the genteel tradition. Those authors who had a natural bent toward romanticism found his prestige valuable in furthering their own cause. The very magnetism and charm of the man were so great as to influence impressionable young men who came within his sphere.

It would be difficult to imagine that Winston Churchill was an exception. Indeed, the author and the President had a number of things in common. Both started out as would-be historians and both glorified the achievements of the American past. Both had a great love for athletics and sports. Both were strong advocates of United States naval preparedness. Both expressed belief in the dominance of the Anglo-Saxons, and they tended to regard American imperialism as a good thing. Abhorring realism, at least in its more extreme phases, both were decidedly romanticists in fiction. Both lent the moral tone to reform. As a matter of fact, both Roosevelt and Churchill thought of themselves essentially as moralists bent on awakening Americans to the need for honesty and to a return to the old traditions in governmental practices. Lastly, both were enthusiasts. There is no doubt that each enjoyed his role in life: Theodore Roosevelt was delighted to be President; Churchill found keen satisfaction as novelist, politician, and preacher.

When Churchill returned from a trip abroad in the spring

of 1902, he decided to run for the Cornish seat in the New Hampshire legislature. After a hard fight, he won the Republican nomination in September and then defeated his Democratic opponent in November. Roosevelt had said, "Get action, do things; don't fritter away your time; create, act, take a place wherever you are and be somebody: get action."[4] Churchill had some ideas about local needs in the Cornish area. Perhaps, after all, he should take his new friend's advice and "get action." He would go to Concord, sit in the legislature, and see what reforms could be accomplished. Actually, the impulse that moved Churchill to enter politics was probably similar to that which motivated many writers of the period to try their hands at political life. Churchill was not unique, therefore, in combining the two roles.

Author Churchill anticipated his first legislative session with all the enthusiasm and determination of a newcomer to politics. He prepared bills to introduce at the January session; he read reports and legislative data covering road and auto regulations in Massachusetts before drawing up similar measures for New Hampshire. He expected results, for the Churchills took a house in Concord and prepared to move there while the legislature met.

What the reaction of the professionals must have been to all this can be surmised. At first, they played along with Churchill. Governor-elect N. J. Bachelder appointed Churchill as a colonel on his staff. The leaders of the party were delighted to have such a big name as Churchill's in their midst. The state government, executive and legislative, was dominated by the Boston and Maine Railroad. The railroad's lobbyists pretty much controlled things in Concord, and they sought to enlist all new legislators to their cause and to educate them to the facts of political life. No doubt, they expected Churchill would be a harmless fellow, so they good-naturedly humored him. The political chieftains appointed him chairman of the House Committee on Forestry, and placed him on the Committee on Public Improvements. These were thought to be innocuous appointments.

Churchill promptly introduced his bills when the session met in January, 1903. All were of a mild, reform nature. He proposed a removal of the toll on the bridge that joined Cornish and Windsor, Vermont (a redemption of a campaign promise);

and he suggested that the Vermont and New Hampshire legislatures work together to provide free bridges across the Connecticut River. Furthermore, he introduced a forestry bill preventing the wholesale denudation of New Hampshire forests by lumbering interests; an education bill requiring the periodic reading of the state and federal constitutions in the public schools; another education bill providing for teaching physiology and hygiene in the schools, with special reference to the effects of stimulants and narcotics (teachers and pupils were to be provided with informative books on these subjects); a bill regulating the speed and operation of automobiles; one providing for a state sanatorium; and a St. Louis Exposition Bill, whereby the state would appropriate fifty thousand dollars for a New Hampshire exhibit at the St. Louis Exposition of 1904. (He had in mind the favorable tourist publicity the state would receive from such an exhibit.) Finally, his interest in history led him to sponsor a resolution to erect a monument at Vicksburg, Mississippi, in honor of the New Hampshire regiments of the Civil War.

With these bills in the hopper and with the apparently innocent belief that they would be promptly enacted into law, Churchill left Concord for a western trip to gather materials for his novel, *The Crossing*. During his absence, the railroad machine ran roughshod over his measures, and he returned to the state in April to find that his favorite bills had met an unfavorable fate. Except for the Vicksburg monument proposal and a modified forestry bill, all his measures had been defeated or had never been considered. The railroad had spoken; Churchill's "reforms" had failed. But he renewed the fight in the next biennial session of the legislature. He was easily elected to his second term in the fall of 1904 and served out the 1905 session in Concord working for further Progressive reforms. By this time, he had entered into full conflict with the Boston and Maine Railroad machine; it was to be the central agitation of his political career.

Churchill told of his rude awakening in politics when he wrote a story for the Boston *Herald* in 1906:

> I went down to Concord and was received most cordially by the politicians. There has never been any question of their cordiality, except when I tried to interfere in politics, and then they told me

firmly but politely that that was forbidden ground for a disinterested citizen. . . . Most of them thought that I had come
down there to get material, and had no idea that I merely
wanted to take my share as a citizen in the government. That was
an unheard of innovation. They did not remember that men of
letters had taken an active part in affairs in the days of Hamilton
and in the days of Emerson. . . . If I tried to talk politics I was
told a funny story. I was not trusted.[5]

Churchill's success as a writer, however, enhanced his position
with the electorate. His activities in the legislature were noted
and recorded nationally. During tours of the West and South in
the spring of 1903 and again in 1906, he was frequently interviewed by newspapermen who inquired about his political career.
And he always commented with exuberance and enthusiasm.
He had caught the full fervor of the Progressive's zeal and was
thoroughly enjoying it.

Consequently, when a group of amateur political reformers
calling themselves the Lincoln Republican Club asked Churchill
to be a candidate for the Republican nomination for governor
in 1906, he obliged. He had been a delegate to the national
Republican convention of 1904 that had renominated Roosevelt;
he had won fame with his activities in the Concord legislature.
Though Churchill was aware of the odds against him, there
seemed to be some hope of success. All during the summer of
1906, he stumped the state for his cause. In accepting the
ᵢchallenge to seek the nomination, he suggested a direct primary
law, another to abolish the lobby system, and one on the lines of
that enacted by the federal government to do away with the
evils of the free-pass system by which the Boston and Maine
Railroad influenced legislators.

Perhaps no state contest was watched with as much nation-
wide interest that summer as the race Churchill waged in New
Hampshire. He had little newspaper endorsement in his own
state, but he had out-of-state interest and support. The Associated
Press carried most of his speeches, and several leading newspapers and magazines of the country carried articles strongly
laudatory of Churchill's stand against the "bossism" of New
Hampshire.[6]

Churchill finally lost the battle—but not until his gallant
effort had thoroughly frightened old-line Republican leaders.

The convention turned out to be a disorganized, riotous gathering. Three other candidates were in the field for the nomination in addition to Churchill. At one time Churchill led in the balloting, but he finally lost out to railroad-endorsed candidate Charles M. Floyd. The railroad machine, however, had undergone the scare of its political life; and the state convention wrote into the platform that year many of the measures the Lincoln Club had sponsored. In a direct primary of voter participation, Churchill would probably have won the nomination, for he was currently a popular vote-getter. But he was up against the caucus; manipulations and combinations were too strong for a political upstart like Churchill to win in 1906.[7]

As a matter of fact, the 1906 election marked the beginning of the end for the railroad. Floyd was elected governor in November by a narrow margin, but many more reform legislators were elected than ever before. Battles ensued, but, by 1910, the Boston and Maine hold on New Hampshire had been broken, most of the reform bills were law, and the Progressives were able to put one of their own number in the governor's chair. Churchill's legislative fights in 1903 and 1905 and his candidacy in 1906 had not been in vain; in fact, *The Outlook* called the latter a "virtual victory."[8] Churchill, who continued to lobby for Lincoln Club measures and the reform planks of the platform, contributed to ridding New Hampshire of one of the worst aspects of early twentieth-century "bossism"—the undue control of legislative matters by railroad interests.

Although his race for the governorship was the last for Churchill until an abortive try on the Bull-Moose Progressive ticket in 1912, he continued to take an active interest in political affairs in the state and nation. He strongly endorsed Roosevelt's measures at the federal level; later, he stumped New Hampshire for the candidacy of Taft in 1908. Since his political beliefs at the time closely paralleled those of Roosevelt, Churchill's early enthusiasm for Taft cooled when Roosevelt became disenchanted with him. By 1912, Churchill, clearly in the Bull-Moose wing of the Republican Party, agreed to run as the Progressive candidate for governor. The result, however, was a reflection of the national picture: the split in Republican ranks enabled a Democrat to win the office.[9]

Like the ex-President he admired, Churchill slipped from the political scene after 1912. But unlike Roosevelt, he felt no great antipathy for Woodrow Wilson. Indeed, though never feeling the close rapport with the Democratic President that he had felt with Roosevelt, Churchill had high regard for Wilson. On two occasions he rented his home in New Hampshire to the Wilsons for a summer White House.[10] Many of the reforms that the Progressives had urged, of course, came to fruition in the first Wilson administration. Although of the opposite political persuasion, Churchill could not help being pleased with the legislative results. But after 1912 his interests in politics were more nearly passive than active.

II

Meanwhile, there were further novels to write. If Churchill had been used occasionally by the political leaders of the New Hampshire machine during his legislative years, it was not altogether a one-way benefit. From state lobbyists and local bosses in Concord, the author heard many stories about "the old days" in politics. Some of the most fascinating tales concerned a former rural political boss, one of the first of his type, named Ruel Durkee. Durkee had come from Croydon, New Hampshire, a hamlet a few miles to the north of Newport and only some twenty miles from Churchill's home in Cornish. A tanner's son, Durkee had, by thrift and Scotch-Irish ability in putting over a deal, accumulated a small amount of money at a rather early age. With native Yankee shrewdness, he then went about buying up mortgages on nearby farms. In time, he became the leading mortgage holder in his section of the state.

With this economic weapon in his hands, he was able to manipulate votes and eventually to work himself up to the position of political boss of the entire state. He would move to Concord during sessions of the legislature (then called the General Court), and there he would manipulate and buy and sell candidates as his particular political deals of the moment required. Unschooled and ignorant, he yet possessed a native shrewdness and uncanny ability at wielding power—a power, incidentally, which he did not always devote to wicked ends. Durkee had his good qualities, and he had his disinterested supporters. But there was no doubt about the questionable methods whereby he achieved and maintained his position. Durkee had died in 1885 when Churchill was just a boy living in St. Louis. The author had never seen the famous man, but in 1903 there were many in Concord who had. From the many anecdotes they told in the hotel rooms and in the legislative chambers, Churchill was able to reproduce Durkee in his own mind and eventually to draw him to near perfection in his next novel.

Coniston deals primarily and psychologically with the life of Jethro Bass, the fictionalized model of Durkee. Son of a rough tanner, Bass grows up among the hills of a certain state in New England that is never named but is clearly New Hampshire. In Coniston, the little town where he lives, young Jethro is regarded with some amusement and disrespect. Reading a biography of Napoleon, Bass is impressed with the way the French emperor compelled men to do his bidding. One is led to believe that the book sets Jethro to thinking about the sweet joys of political power. "Existing conditions presented themselves, and it occurred to him that there were crevices in the town system, and ways into power through the crevices for men clever enough to find them."[11] Saving up money from his tannery expeditions to Boston, Bass buys up the mortgages of numerous nearby farmers. Eventually his aim is recognized by the townspeople; and, instead of being a source of amusement, he becomes the object of considerable distrust and fear. Indeed, when Jethro rounds up all the Jackson Democrats in Coniston and organizes them to get himself elected selectman (the only political office he ever held), it is thought by the respectable Whigs that his soul may have already gone to the Devil and that he is quite beyond Christian redemption.

Bass is in love with Cynthia Ware, daughter of the town minister and a girl of much discernment and some social station. Far above Jethro culturally, she nevertheless feels an attraction for him and learns to love him for the strength she sees in him. She feels he has a force that, if properly channeled, may take him far in life. It is Cynthia who first buys him the biography of Napoleon to read, although she scarcely recognizes the things it may suggest to him. As Bass prepares to gain political control of the town of Coniston by his devious methods, Cynthia surmises what he is about. One night just before the crucial town meeting at which Jethro is elected chairman of the selectmen, she comes to him to implore him to desist. But he has gone too far; he cannot stop now: "What she asked was impossible. That wind which he himself had loosed, which was to topple over institutions, was rising, and he could no more have stopped it then than he could have hushed the storm."[12] In short, Jacksonian Democracy was on the march in Yankee New Hampshire. Cynthia Ware leaves him in anger, never to see him again. She goes to Boston, where she marries a kind but weak man named William Wetherell.

Churchill then leaps over the years to the post-Civil War era. Cynthia Wetherell has died; her husband, ill and broken himself, brings his daughter, also named Cynthia, back to Coniston, of which he had heard so much from his wife. There he buys a small store, and Bass eventually gets the mortgage. Bass is now at the height of his power. During the Civil War, he has switched political parties to become a stalwart Republican. From the Throne Room of the Pelican Hotel at the capital, he rules the state's General Court sessions: "This legislature sat to him as a sort of advisory committee of three hundred and fifty; an expensive advisory committee to the people, relic of an obsolete form of government."[13] In one hilarious but revealing chapter called "The Woodchuck Session," Churchill shows how shrewdly Bass maneuvers to get his favorite measures passed. It is one of the best chapters Churchill ever wrote. Bass has an elaborate system of local lieutenants throughout the state who hold mortgages and who fit into the unique political machine he has built. They are completely at his beck and call. "Don't write, send!" he warns whenever he wishes to summon one of them. Many of these lieutenants were painted from life by Churchill as he portrayed an aspect of local politics that he had learned only too well in his own campaigns.

Jethro's love for Cynthia Ware never leaves him, although he marries a colorless ornament whom he makes for purposes of show the best-dressed woman in the state. The love he had for the girl of his youth is now transferred to the daughter, Cynthia Wetherell. Because of this affection, he befriends Wetherell and eventually supports him, not only financially but in the coveted literary career Wetherell seeks, since it is through Bass's influence that some of Wetherell's pieces are printed in local papers.

Eventually, Wetherell's illness that had brought him to Coniston in the first place causes his death. Jethro Bass then adopts the daughter, Cynthia, who grows up adoring him, since she is ignorant of the past and of the political methods of her foster father.

At this point the second political issue is introduced. The new opponent and enemy of Bass is Isaac D. Worthington, who has made a fortune in his nearby Brampton textile mill. A philanthropist who has contributed generously to the civic improvement of Brampton, Worthington typifies the new type of postwar businessman; he is ruthless in his own desire for power and wealth, yet eager to curry public favor by heavily endowing local charities. Gradually, he has put his money into the control and ownership of railroads. Eventually he reaches the point where he wishes to consolidate the western railroads of the state to insure his financial and economic success. This ambition, however, brings him into conflict with Jethro Bass, who is still a potent political boss and opposed to such a consolidation. A political fight to the death ensues which is really a test between continued boss rule or railroad domination of the state.

Jethro wins the first round of the fight which centers in the appointment of a postmaster at Brampton. At this one point in the book, Churchill switches to the national level when he has Bass journey to Washington to arrange a "chance" meeting between his postmaster candidate, Ephraim Prescott, and President Grant. Prescott, a veteran of the Civil War Wilderness campaign, soon captures the sympathy of Grant in their reminiscing moments and the President intercedes in behalf of Bass's man. This clever tactic, underhanded in Worthington's none too valid judgment, further infuriates the railroad magnate against Jethro.

Meanwhile, Cynthia Wetherell has been sent by Bass to a fashionable young ladies' school in Boston. There she meets and falls in love with Isaac Worthington's son Robert, a student at Harvard. Newspaper reports about Bass's political manipulations fall into her hands. A young lady with a considerable conscience, she is so greatly disturbed that she goes back to Coniston to see if the things said about "Uncle Jethro" are true. Confronted with her questions, Bass confesses, and a scene ensues which is almost a repetition of the earlier incident between the young

Bass and Cynthia's mother, Cynthia Ware. To please young "Cynthy," whose love and affection he values more than his political power, he agrees to withdraw from the political arena and to give up his fight with Isaac Worthington. Cynthia decides to leave Jethro's guardianship, largely to add to the penance he must do for his political wrongs. However, she takes a teaching position in Brampton where she will not be too far away from her beloved "Uncle Jethro."

Worthington now makes a fatal move. When he learns that the adopted daughter of his arch-enemy, Bass, is employed as a teacher in Brampton, he uses his influence to have her discharged. Furthermore, he is so incensed when he learns that his son is in love with this woman that he forbids a proposed marriage and any further meeting. These actions so anger Jethro Bass that he forthwith determines to re-enter the political lists, Cynthia or no Cynthia, for one last time. Returning to the state capital, he gathers his forces and soon makes it known to Worthington that there will be no Consolidation Bill unless he comes to terms with his old enemy. The price he demands is Worthington's consent to the marriage of Cynthia and Bob, a price Worthington reluctantly pays to gain railroad control: "The price was indeed heavy—the heaviest he could pay. But the alternative—was not that heavier? To relinquish his dream of power, to sink for a while into a crippled state; for he had spent large sums, and one of those periodical depressions had come to the business of the mills, and those Western investments were not looking so bright now." As for Jethro, "For this girl's sake, [he] was willing to forego his revenge, was willing at the end of his days to allow the world to believe that he had sold out to his enemy, or that he had been defeated by him."[14]

This is Bass's last political act, his last victory. As he gazes out the window of the Throne Room at the Pelican after the meeting with Worthington that has sealed the bargain, he muses on this final stratagem: "Perhaps he was thinking of the life he had lived, which was spent now: of the men he had ruled, of the victories he had gained from that place which would know him no more. . . . Perhaps he looked back over the highway of his life and thought of the woman whom he had loved, and wondered what it would have been if she had trod it by his side. Who will judge him? He had been what he had been; and as the

Era was, so was he. Verily, one generation passeth away, and another generation cometh."[15] Thus, Churchill uses Bass as a symbol for the earlier boss era which is superseded by the new corporation rule.

The ending of the book is unsatisfactory to a modern reader, but it acceded to the happy-ending tastes of 1906. "I like to dwell on happiness," Churchill wrote.[16] Cynthia and Bob are married, and Jethro lives out his life playing with their children and basking in his memories. But at the same time, the conclusion is immoral, for Jethro Bass has betrayed the state by turning it over to the railroad power. Churchill has so condemned Worthington and his kind during the course of the novel and has so sentimentalized Bass and converted him from a villain into a penitent hero that one worries about Bass's replacement in the political arena. The rule of the Worthingtons promises no good for the public. The happy ending Churchill thought he had written is beclouded with this unanswered question; the reader fears the evil days to come.

The publication of *Coniston* coincided with Churchill's 1906 campaign for the governorship. Unquestionably, the novel helped his political fortunes and brought him the attention of the public. The Lincoln Republican Club thought *Coniston* was the *Uncle Tom's Cabin* of politics and that it would awaken public interest generally to the dangers of the Worthington-type railroad rule that the Boston and Maine illustrated. On the other hand, his political race that summer helped place the book on the best-seller list for 1906.[17]

An immediate success, *Coniston* had gone into its fifth large printing two months after its initial publication in June. The book held its appeal through Macmillan editions in 1912, 1925, and 1927; the English edition also enjoyed a wide sale. As late as the 1940's, it was still being read in some schools as a picture of the New England social scene before and after the Civil War. Although the book did not enjoy the tremendous popularity of the historical romances (only one of Churchill's later novels did), it was a decided financial success.

High praise, and a few dissenting voices, came from the reviewers. The *Atlantic Monthly, North American Review,* and *Review of Reviews* thought Churchill had returned to his earlier good form.[18] "The most substantial and craftsmanlike piece of work Mr. Churchill has yet produced," said the *Atlantic*. James MacArthur in *Harper's Weekly* gave the book mild praise, although he was inclined to think that much of Churchill's popularity was due to the passion for patriotism of the times.[19] Interestingly, some English journals in their enthusiasm now voiced the opinion that the name of the American Winston Churchill would be remembered long after that of the Englishman had been forgotten. *Coniston* also won plaudits from many people engaged in the national fight for reform. Theodore Roosevelt and Albert Beveridge were among those who endorsed the book and its message.

One of the most significant things about *Coniston* for today's reader is the way in which it perfectly illustrates the moral tone of righteous optimism that characterized Rooseveltian Progressivism down to about 1908. The Concord *Daily Patriot* observed that "*Coniston* should delight President Roosevelt, for while it deals unsparingly with the evils of American politics, it breathes a wholesome optimism and a hope for the ultimate triumph of representative government in its best aspect. . . . As American citizens we must take to heart the political lesson so subtly taught. . . . This small volume contains all the essential features which are elaborately described by James Bryce in *The American Commonweath*."[20] The optimism that the *Daily Patriot* found so abundant in the book was central to Roosevelt Progressivism during its first phase.

Certainly, the early aim of the Progressives was not for something new, for something different or unique in the political structure. Alfred Kazin has described Progressivism as "nostalgic": "The muckraker's apotheosis was always the same—a vision of small, quiet lives humbly and usefully led; a transcription of Jeffersonian small-village ideals for a generation bound to megalopolis, yet persistently nostalgic for the old-fashioned peace and the old-fashioned ideal."[21] Actually, the Progressives advocated a *return* to the older ways of representative government that old-fashioned idealism had nurtured. Disgusted with the concentration of wealth and political power in the hands of the trusts and their henchmen, the bosses, the Progressives suggested a remedy in a return to honest government of the people. Capitalism and democracy, in the Progressive mind, were essentially sound systems; but they had been prostituted by monopoly and corruption. The Progressives wanted to sweep corrupt men from office, break up concentrated power in the form of trusts and combines, and restore genuine free enterprise. A moral regeneration was what was needed, and the ways of the founding fathers should be an example for the restoration of morality and integrity to government.

This is precisely the moral solution that *Coniston* implies. In his "Afterword" to the book, Churchill had written:

> Self-examination is necessary for the moral health of nations as well as men, and it is the most hopeful of signs that in the United States we are to-day going through a period of self-examination. . . . In America to-day we are trying—whatever the cost—to regain the true axis established for us by the founders of our Republic.[22]

By righting itself and "regaining the true axis," the nation might remedy its ills. Bass had been dethroned; his era had passed. If the people could defeat the corporation trusts, as exemplified in the railroad, or clear them of their dishonest masters, all would be well. Perhaps better than any other current novel, *Coniston* clearly indicates this first moderate phase of Progressivism; and, though it is largely confined to the state level, the author asserts that "the conditions here depicted, while retaining the characteristics of the locality, [are] typical of the Era over a large part of the United States."[23]

Fictionally, *Coniston* is important because it presents the best character that Churchill ever drew. A New Hampshire "David Harum," Jethro Bass lives in the mind long after the book has been read. Although there were some in Churchill's day who protested that Bass was unreal, most of the protestations were motivated by political pressures or nostalgic friendship for Ruel Durkee. Most impartial observers agreed that Churchill had drawn Durkee accurately. Fred L. Pattee, a native of New Hampshire, has commented: "By no means did the author overdraw him. The actual Ruel Durkee *did* become the state dictator and he *did* say that he carried the State of New Hampshire in his vest pocket, and there was truth in what he said. And even now his crudities and his rural philosophy are remembered and quoted."[24] If Durkee lives at all, it will be in Churchill's admirable portrait of Bass.

Churchill did well, too, with some of the minor characters in the novel. Lucretia Penniman, a spinster, but nonetheless a conqueror, may have been patterned after Sarah Josepha Hale: "—Lucretia Penniman, one of the first to sound the clarion note for the intellectual independence of American women; who wrote the 'Hymn to Coniston'; who, to the awe of her townspeople, went out into the great world and became editress of a famous women's journal, and knew Longfellow and Hawthorne and Bryant."[25] Cynthia Wetherell is one of the better Churchill heroines. 'Bijah Bixby is a genuine comic character and profoundly typical of his kind. Indeed, *Coniston* has a pleasant element of humor that had been lacking in the earlier romances.

The picture of rural New England is good. Truer to the region's life than Edith Wharton's or Eugene O'Neill's portraits, the book stands closer to the local color delineations of Sarah Orne Jewett or of Mary E. Wilkins Freeman. The characters and the settings are authentic. Churchill, who had studied New Englanders with a fondness that his own lineage dictated, captured their peculiarities, their strong points, and their faults with remarkable insight. A resident of New Hampshire for barely eight years, Churchill made it his country in *Coniston*.[26]

Finally, *Coniston* is less diffuse than the historical novels preceding it. In this respect, at least, it is the best book Churchill ever wrote; only *A Modern Chronicle* (1910) stands comparison with it on this point. One of Churchill's great fictional weaknesses had been the lack of coherent plot structure. Almost all his novels had been episodic, inchoate in form. In *Coniston* he corrected this fault, though he later fell back into the same error of structure with succeeding novels. The book is a tightly knit story and, on the whole, is a highly successful example of the novelist's craft.

Churchill's romantic tendency to sentimentalize, however, is not corrected in *Coniston*. Perhaps he can be excused as a product of the age, for almost all the other political novels popular during the period were equally sentimental. Realism and naturalism had entered fiction when Churchill was writing; but, as already noted, at the time he did not approve of these newer, fresher literary currents. The same shopworn, faultless hero and spotless heroine furnish the love story; circumstance again plays its fortuitous role; there is the usual eagerness for the happy ending. The author's own personality intrudes too often with frequent annoying "asides" to the reader. The real villian, Isaac Worthington, is the incarnation of villainy—what at this time Churchill was beginning to consider the worst type in society, the self-seeking businessman. Only Jethro Bass is a composite of black and white. Even with him, at the very end, sentiment gets the better of the author. Bass's recantation, morally admirable as it may be, deprives him of much of the force and the strength that make him a living figure. After all, there is scarcely a more sentimental character in fiction than the would-be scoundrel whose rough exterior hides a heart of gold.

Yet, *Coniston* lives largely because of its portrait of Jethro Bass. Whether Churchill had drawn Durkee to perfection or not, he had written an admirable portrait of the Jacksonian rural political boss. "The Era of the first six Presidents had closed," Churchill wrote, "and a new Era had begun. I am speaking of political Eras. Certain gentlemen, with a pious belief in democracy, but with a firmer determination to get on top, arose—and got on top. So many of these gentlemen arose in the different states, and they were so clever, and they found so many chinks in the Constitution to crawl through and steal the people's chestnuts, that the Era may be called the Boss-Era."[27] An exponent of Jacksonian politics, of the "might makes right" theory, Bass is an example of a figure that flourished along with the broader democracy that the Jacksonian Era ushered in. As a fictional character or as an historical type, he is well worth knowing. Morris E. Speare may have exaggerated when he said, "As a contribution to the permanent figures of American literature, [Bass] takes his place among the best and the most significant creations of American writers." But he did not exaggerate when he called *Coniston* "the best chronicle we have, in American literature, of the old-time state boss."[28]

III

With both *Coniston* and his summer campaign for the gubernatorial nomination out of the way in the fall of 1906, Churchill turned his attention to his next venture in fiction. Within a few weeks, he had decided upon a fictional account of his governorship battle of the summer before. "I had gone to the

New Hampshire Legislature and had been a candidate for governor," Churchill reported years later. "*Mr. Crewe's Career* in particular was more or less autobiographical. I like to think that I was making fun, perhaps more or less unconsciously, of myself."29

Mr. Crewe's Career was published in May, 1908. A political novel, it dealt with the contemporary railroad rulers in a state obviously New Hampshire. During 1906, Churchill probably did not realize that he was again accumulating material for a novel; for he had conducted his campaign for the nomination in all earnestness, not to seek source material for fiction. But by 1907 that campaign seemed, in retrospect, highly significant and not a little amusing. It proved to be the well-spring of a diverting tale and of a serious exposé.

The main action of *Mr. Crewe's Career* revolves around Humphrey Crewe's campaign for governor. Like Churchill in 1906, Crewe seeks his party's nomination for that high office, he finances his own campaign, and he is a wealthy amateur in politics whose first efforts are bungling, even ludicrous. In fact, Crewe starts out as a rather pompous fool, but he grows with political experience into a shrewd manipulator for reform. Churchill later intimated that he was parodying himself in his portrayal of Crewe. Although other people thought they saw other prototypes for the fictional hero, Churchill denied them all. It is very apparent that Crewe learns about the state's politics and particularly its railroad machine in precisely the same fashion that Churchill did.

But though he gives the title to the book, Crewe is really not the main character; he is rather a burlesque figure of comic relief. One of the main characters is Judge Hilary Vane, the shrewd, able lawyer who is the railroad's legal counsel in the state. At once a statesman, politician, lawyer, and gentleman of old New England ancestry, Vane is the power behind the governor's chair, the manipulator of nominations, the lobbyist who dictates what bills' may pass at sessions of the legislature.

Hilary Vane has a lawyer son, Austen, who has spent some time in the Western states where he has learned the ways of vigor and of clean, open fighting. Austen returns from his sojourn in the West to take up the lawsuit of a poor farmer who has been injured in an accident clearly caused by railroad negligence. This case brings Austen into open conflict with his father, and it gives Churchill a chance to expose one of the prime evils of the Boston and Maine Railroad in New Hampshire —its failure to provide safety devices at crossings and its habit of buying off the accident victims (or their surviving relatives) at a much smaller sum than an impartial law court would award them.

Churchill soon brings Austen Vane to an even greater clash with his father. Pointing to the original act that permitted the consolidation of the Northeastern Railroads, Austen reminds his father that the measure prohibited any increase of railroad rates, passenger or freight. But quite contrary to this law, rates had steadily increased for almost twenty years. He suggests that one of his clients, the Gaylord Lumber Company, is prepared to sue for recovery of the money paid the railroad in increased lumber freight rates and to seek a remedy to railroad violation of the unamended statute. His father, after suggesting that it is too late now to make recovery, falls back on the old "Book of Arguments" and accuses Austen of conniving to attack sacred property rights which are "the foundation of the State's prosperity."[30]

In pointing to this railroad rate problem, Churchill called the attention of the people of New Hampshire to a similar law in their own state passed in 1889. For some reason, the measure had gone unnoticed. One of the effects of *Mr. Crewe's Career* was to focus public notice on this act and to aid in forcing the attorney-general of the state to bring suit against the Boston and Maine Railroad for violations of the forgotten statute. The railroad did not deny that it had broken the law, but it did maintain that it was too late to do anything about it.[31]

Meanwhile, in the novel, Austen meets and falls in love with the daughter of railroad president Augustus Flint, the most powerful character in the book and the most sinister. Many years before, Flint had served under Isaac Worthington, the railroad leader of *Coniston;* from Worthington, he had learned all that gentleman's business philosophy and his worst unethical practices. From his New York offices, Flint rules the Northeastern Railroad that dominates the state. His daughter Victoria, however, is of different moral fibre, although she has all her father's robustness and strength of character. Beautiful and high-minded, she rejects the courtship of Austen at first; but, like all Churchill heroines, she leaves the door ajar and is not too vigorous in her protests.

This romantic love story is bound up with Humphrey Crewe's campaign for governor. Crewe has served in the legislature where many of his worthy bills were killed by the railroad's agents. He thereupon decided to conduct a reform campaign in opposition to the Northeastern's domination. To begin with, he is supported only by an Anglophile society woman, Mrs. Patterson Pomfret, who wants to bring the level of state politics up to that of the Conservative gentlemen in the British Parliament. Slowly, his political effort, laughed at by all except women, gains momentum; it soon appears that he will be a serious threat for the nomination.[32]

Hilary Vane, as the railroad's agent, must prevent at all costs the nomination of Crewe. At the same time, some of the best people in the state have urged Austen Vane to seek the nomination on a reform platform. Young Vane is torn by his loyalty to his aging father, his desire for honest government, his own opposition to the Northeastern's tactics, and his love for Augustus Flint's daughter. At the last moment, after the convention has actually been called to order, he gives a final "no" to the movement to nominate him.

The description of the convention itself is drawn almost entirely from Churchill's recollection of the New Hampshire Republican convention of September, 1906. Pandemonium reigns, illegal votes are taken, illegal delegates are rushed in at crucial moments. Crewe comes near to winning the nomination, but he is finally defeated by the railroad's candidate, "The Honourable Giles Henderson," when Hilary Vane makes the greatest effort of his political career in manipulating his henchmen.

This superb act in the service of railroad executive Flint is Vane's last, however. Suffering from heart trouble, but plagued even more now with doubts about his own conduct, Hilary Vane resigns his post with the Northeastern Railroad; his twinge of conscience is largely due to Austen's arguments.[33] Austen takes his father's message of resignation, along with important railroad papers, to Flint after the convention. The ensuing scene is the high point of the book from the standpoint of Churchill's Progressive philosophy. Standing before Flint, Austen indicts the corrupt practices of the railroad and sounds the note of reforming hope. He warns Flint that the railroad's ability to elect governors and to dictate legislation is becoming a thing of the past, since the people will no longer tolerate political domination by corporations. Flint accuses Austen of being a radical and argues that the nation has changed materially from the utopian days of its founding. The old ideals, he says, will no longer work in the twentieth century. Austen counters with the moral emphasis of the Progressives. He acknowledges that the country has changed materially, but asserts it has not changed morally. The principles upon which the nation was founded must be preserved, for if the American experiment fails, the material interests of which Flint is so solicitous will prove valueless. Thus Churchill's solution to the dilemma of the time is to put faith in the electorate to justify matters in regard to the vested interests, and to return to the idealism of the past.

As for the story itself, Hilary and his son Austen are reconciled by the father's action. Austen wins his girl, despite his quarrel with her father. Indeed, even old Flint accepts the marriage with good grace, recognizing Austen's courage and letting things stand with an agreement to disagree.

Mr. Crewe's Career was dedicated "to the men who in every state of the Union are engaged in the struggle for purer politics." But the book failed to arouse the enthusiasm that *Coniston* did, perhaps because railroad exposure was already nearly complete. New Hampshire political figures were now too sullen to comment about a Churchill novel. In general, the book did not enjoy the popularity of Churchill's first political effort in fiction. And sales fell well below the records set by the three historical novels.

Yet, *Mr. Crewe's Career* was by no means a failure. It led the *Bookman* lists for 1908 as the number one best-seller, the fourth Churchill book to enjoy that distinction. Macmillan had later editions in 1924 and 1927, Grosset and Dunlap's cheap editions came out in 1912 and 1913, there were the usual English and Canadian editions, and a German translation was printed in 1909. A poor seller for Churchill might mean a best-seller for almost any other author.

Churchill's friends were impressed with the novel, and

criticisms of *Mr. Crewe's Career* in the journals and newspapers were generally favorable, although some publications that had always reviewed his novels when they appeared did not take notice of this second political story. Writers in the *Dial* and the *Independent* made particularly perceptive comments in their reviews. One found the book embodied a wholesome lesson, and the other observed that "the story is of great value for enlightening the great mass of people who are not sufficiently interested in their citizenship to insure honest government, but who are sufficiently interested in the romance to take lessons in political economy from the pen of a novelist."[34] Churchill was indeed passing on to the more didactic fiction of the problem novel.

Mr. Crewe's Career is inferior to *Coniston* as a work of fiction. The characters, again, as in so many of the historical romances, are types, representatives of the ideas the author wished to illustrate. None of them lives beyond a first reading. The plot is sentimental romance. At the end, Austen and Victoria disappear in the yellow gold of an autumn evening, with a bequest from old Hilary Vane that enables them to make a honeymoon tour of the ruins of Europe. Hilary Vane's repentance, itself, is scarcely believable. Churchill's conclusions about the future of corporation rule are too naïve and optimistic. The novel does have more humor than most Churchill creations, but this only seems to add to its triviality.

However, *Mr. Crewe's Career* is better than *Coniston* as a political tract. A novel with a didactic purpose, it exposes the power of the corporation in state politics and presses the question left unanswered at the end of *Coniston*. Illegal lobbying, the manipulations of railroad interests in state governments, the evils of the free-pass system, the corruption of able young lawyers through offers of political preferment, the practices of favors and rebates to selected shippers, the power of the railroad over the press, the entire ugly framework within which the "vested interests" worked—all these aspects of post-Civil War America are revealed in their naked boldness.

Yet, *Mr. Crewe's Career* is no plea for agitators. With all the exposed corruption, the implication is clear that gentlemen of social position, of integrity, and of gentility must lead the way to the correction of abuses. This, of course, was another article of faith Churchill held in common with some other members of the Progressive movement. The older figures in the novel's political drama are never to be too severely condemned, for at no time does Austen Vane really consider his father dishonest or corrupt; he sees him more as a misguided victim of an outmoded system. "We mustn't blame the railroads too severely, when they grew strong enough, for substituting their own political army to avoid being blackmailed."[35] Just as much as *Coniston, Mr. Crewe's Career* illustrates the moderation of the Progressive attitude of President Roosevelt.

Since both *Coniston* and *Mr. Crewe's Career* are good representations of Progressivism, the books are of value for a contemporary reader. Of the Roosevelt Progressives, Richard Hofstadter writes: "Their criticisms of American society were, in their utmost reaches, very searching and radical, but they were themselves moderate men who intended to propose no radical remedies. From the beginning . . . they were limited by the disparity between the boldness of their means and the tameness of their ends. They were working at a time of widespread prosperity, and their chief appeal was not to desperate social needs but to mass sentiments of responsibility, indignation, and guilt. Hardly anyone intended that these sentiments should result in action drastic enough to transform American society."[36] The main issue of both *Coniston* and *Mr. Crewe's Career* is not for sweeping reforms to remedy a faltering democratic system. The judgment is that the sorry condition of affairs of the state or of the nation is the people's fault because they permit it to exist. Graft is the price the public pays for political negligence. The political novelists, on the whole, were simply trying to awaken the people to their responsibilities in meeting the issues of arbitrary power. To remind the public that things do not run of themselves and to encourage the virtue and wisdom of the people were the purposes of Churchill's fictional messages.

Mr. Crewe's Career illustrates another Progressive trait: the optimism of Austen Vane is characteristic of that of the reformers in general. Austen is convinced that a new political day is dawning—an indication that Churchill may have felt that the political times were improving. But, for the most part, such optimism proved premature. The Progressives after 1908 were forced to turn to more serious economic changes as the answer to the troubles of their times—and Winston Churchill is an adequate illustration of this trend. As Theodore Roosevelt altered his views after he left the presidency and moved into a more radical position, and as Progressivism took on its economic tinge through the influence of men like Robert La Follette and Louis Brandeis, Churchill's novels reflected the change. It is perhaps a gauge of his movement toward the left and farther from the central position of many Americans that he began to lose some of his enormous reading public. His later economic and social-problem novels did not achieve the popularity of either the historical romances or the two political books. Progressivism in 1912 could not elect its candidate; by 1916, it was largely defunct as a party. Churchill's next novels revealed this pattern, for he began to move farther from the main pulse of the nation and closer to the position of the national Progressive Party. *Coniston* and *Mr. Crewe's Career* were illustrations of the first phase of Progressivism; the later novels were to illustrate the second, more drastic, but probably more discerning aspects of the movement.

CHAPTER 4

The Emerging Social Critic:
Modern Marriage and Divorce

B Y THE END of the second Theodore Roosevelt administration in 1908, the early Progressive reforms had largely been accomplished. Corrupt men had been swept from office, municipal clean-up campaigns were in full swing, anti-trust suits had been instituted, conservation measures had been enacted. The first fruits of the muckrakers' efforts were being tested. The emphasis on a return to the ideals of the founders had had time to be tried in the crucible of practical politics. With the rascals turned out and with supposedly honest men possessing the disinterestedness of the forefathers everywhere in their places, content apparently should have reigned.

That such was not the case, farmers, labor groups, and liberals were soon to attest. The reformers, who earlier had advocated mildness and moderation, now turned more searching eyes on the economic and social structure of the country. Many of them became rather perceptive social critics, as they studied the new sciences of sociology, economics, and social psychology. Among the texts they perused were the books of Thorstein Veblen, Lester Ward, and Richard Ely; and La Follette's "Wisconsin Idea" served as the practical model of their application. The result of all this was a change in Progressive emphasis on the role of government in a reform society. The old moral argument of the government as an umpire no longer seemed adequate. The new Progressivism looked instead to direct government intervention and regulation to effect changes in the economy and society—something new under the American political sun.

Roosevelt himself reflected the change. His tenure as President had borne out the moral tone; his campaign on the Progressive ticket in 1912 clearly reflected another note, the strong government thesis. The 1912 speeches of Churchill in New Hampshire, representative of national Progressivism, showed the concern with newer economic and social problems. Poverty, child labor, unemployment insurance, unbridled laissez-faire business tactics, and an outmoded Constitution were now the subjects of the author's thought. His own interests were indicative of the changing emphasis that national Progressivism had undergone.

It was inevitable that, as the Progressive mind truly became "progressive," it should take a close look at social problems. The fiction of the Progressive era reflected the trend, for there was a continuing decline in popularity of the historical romance and the political novel, and a gradual development of the new novel concerned with some current social issue. This change in the Progressive viewpoint between 1908 and 1912 tended to focus Churchill's attention directly on such subjects as the place of the "New Woman" in American society, the influence of Christian Socialism and the social gospel on the business community in particular and on modern government in general, and the difficulties attendant on the rise of modern industry. For ten years after 1908, Churchill's fiction dealt, therefore, with these various problems brought about by the changing era.

One of the first problems some of the leading writers considered was the rise of the so-called "New Woman" in American life. The increased freedom women were enjoying; the competition they were beginning to provide in the professions and the trades; the constant and growing agitation for woman suffrage; and, above all, the increased divorce rate interested many novelists and annoyed others. Divorce itself was no new topic for the American novel, but between 1908 and World War I the subject was revived and exploited in a number of magazine articles and works of fiction.[1] Progressive novelists like David Graham Phillips and Robert Herrick turned to it; the genteel James Lane Allen did also. Among the women writers Edith Wharton and Mary Austin were to follow suit. In 1908, Churchill turned his thoughts in a similar direction.

Devoting his extra energies only to political affairs in the early fall, Churchill worked on his new book until December, when he temporarily abandoned it for a midwinter vacation in the South. But he returned to the novel in earnest the following spring; and all during the summer and fall of 1909, amidst his political activities, he continued with the writing. By Christmas he had finished the book. Leaving the manuscript with his publishers, he sailed in December for Europe on the *Lusitania* for a tour that was to take him eventually to the Nile Valley.

A Modern Chronicle, published in March, 1910, is really the first of the four Churchill problem novels. It is a novel of divorce—but it is more than that. It is also a tract attacking the Spencerian "survival of the fittest" theory in business and American materialism in the marriage relationship. Honora Leffingwell, heroine of the book, is beautiful, innocent, and clever after a fashion; but she is avid for all things that go to make a luxurious, amusing life. More particularly, she craves the happiness that she thinks money and exalted social station can bring. The book, essentially, is the story of her search for these ends and the disillusionment that follows their achievement.

Born abroad in the last quarter of the nineteenth century, Honora is the daughter of a pair of Americans possessing a gift for the good things of this world, but they have no sterling traits of character to bequeath to their child. Her father, Randolph Leffingwell, a St. Louisan, had been United States consul at Nice. Of aristocratic Southern birth, he bore himself in the manner of royalty. Beauty and a knowledge of the social graces had been the distinguishing characteristics of the mother. Also of Southern blood, she had married the consul against her father's wish, since he had taken her to Paris to choose a count or a duke. Churchill makes much of this hereditary strain in Honora, but he does so more by implication than direct statement since only the first chapter, "What's In Heredity," is directly devoted to it.

When Honora's parents are killed in an accident along the Riviera while the child is still an infant, she is brought to America and handed over to her uncle, Tom Leffingwell, and his wife, Aunt Mary, a childless couple living in St. Louis on a modest income. It is not precisely in poverty that Honora is brought up, but certainly in conditions unfavorable to gorgeous display. But Honora is indulged a great deal—too much for her own good. Adored by her relatives, she is spoiled and coddled;

and at fourteen she is already selfish, beautiful, temperamental. She is, above all, ambitious, and has determined to seek a higher social plane than prosaic St. Louis can offer. Churchill points out that ideas and material ambitions commonly held by American women had taken possession of her. Faithful, loyal, steady Peter Erwin, who one soon realizes is to be the stock hero of this book, is no match for her dreams of a prince gallant who will lead her up the social ladder.

Escape promises when at seventeen Honora is sent East to Sutcliffe, a fashionable girls' boarding school. There she has "a glimpse of the world." She readily accepts an invitation from her wealthy roommate, Susan Holt, to visit the Holt summer establishment at Silverdale during a vacation period. There her ambitions are whetted by a procession of eligible young males, and in one day she receives three proposals: one from a rising young member of the New York Stock Exchange; one from a French vicomte; and one from dogged Peter Erwin, who has followed her to Silverdale to advance his suit at this late date. Her ambitions dictate that she accept the member of the stock exchange, Howard Spence, and a marriage is arranged.

But the union proves to be a mistake. The Spences move to a dreary New Jersey suburb, Rivington. It immediately develops that Spence's financial star has not quite risen yet,. though he enters the Wall Street combat with all the energy at his command. His one interest in life is money, but Honora at least pretends that she is concerned with higher things. The Rivington scenes are a damning commentary on suburban life and the damaging family relationship that results from a commuter existence. Spence lives in the business world, leaving his wife to her own dreams, which are definitely for a better social set than Rivington offers.

As the years pass, Spence grows bald and fat, and Honora threatens finally to leave him. To placate her, they move to a fashionable place on Long Island, symbolically named Quicksands. Here a fast and vulgar set exists in perpetual bridge games, tennis matches, teas, and formal dinners—the 1910 version of the modern cocktail set. Honora is attracted by the rich Trixy Brent, who introduces her to an even faster, smarter, richer group of people in New York. She thinks she has found her ideal in Brent, for she is charmed by his smart ways, his quick banter.

But shortly she finds that he is seeking to compromise her; and, after a mildly explosive scene in which she rejects his suggestions, Honora breaks off their relationship. (This was the first time Churchill had even skirted the idea of illicit love in his novels, but he was to turn to it more openly in later books.)

The Spences then move to a house in New York, growing ever richer and farther apart. Howard is now completely absorbed in the struggles of the financial world which he regards in terms of the Darwinian survival of the fittest. Honora is invited into the wealthy set at Newport for the summer, where she meets a veritable Viking of a fellow, Hugh Chiltern. Chiltern, a dynamic man, immediately sweeps her off her feet. Tall, handsome, forceful, inclined to indulge visions of crusading ventures into politics (always in the future, however), he seems to offer everything that Howard Spence does not have. In a passionate swirl, Honora decides to divorce her fat broker husband and to marry Chiltern. When she faces Howard with this prospect, he quite correctly reminds her that when she married him she had visions of fine houses and fancy parties. She had, indeed, been quite satisfied to marry Prosperity. She does not deny this and acknowledges that her earlier standards had been false. But she maintains that now her values have changed; she sees that there are things in life more important than mere material prosperity. She accuses Howard of not loving her; and, adopting a moral tone, she indicts his business practices, which she feels are wholly unethical—though this thought apparently had not occurred to her when she was seeking to scale the moneyed world herself.[2]

Honora goes through with her divorce, although she has doubts about what the social world may think of her actions, particularly the worlds of St. Louis and of Chiltern into which she is moving. But she hopes that the notoriety surrounding her divorce will gradually die down and that people will forget. When Churchill takes his heroine to Reno and shows how the divorce mill works, it is clear that he holds an attitude of the highest reproach for her action.

Honora and Hugh are then married and retire to his ancestral Pennsylvania estate of "Grenoble." There she hopes to start her new life, to follow in the noble footsteps of Hugh's mother as mistress of his home. Envisioning patterns of order and responsibility in her new role, she sees herself as the wife of the local magnate, the social leader of the community, the respected bride of old General Chiltern's son.

For a short summertime things go fairly well. But soon Chiltern shows signs of boredom; it is not his nature to be long satisfied in one place. Honora is obliged to adopt all kinds of strategems to retain her new husband's love. The break comes when the people of the community revolt and refuse to accept her socially because of the stigma of her notorious divorce. They snub her on every occasion; they even reject her efforts to join in local church and philanthropic endeavors. Honora, who then realizes her original misgivings were prophetic, confesses her mistake and acknowledges her own selfishness in marrying Hugh. Chiltern's reaction to this social pressure is to turn villain. He flies into dark rages, disappears for periods of dissolute living, and frequently takes out his torment on Honora herself. Finally, he is killed when he is thrown from a vicious horse—an act of semi-suicide, Churchill implies. Honora is left free to contemplate in remorse the folly of her two marriages.

For four years she withdraws from the world and undergoes a cleansing of soul, while subsisting on an income Chiltern had left her. In the final chapter, she is living a secluded life in Paris. Again, Churchill, who could not escape "the romantic compromise,"[3] drags in the happy ending. A Dreiser would have left her in her apartments across the Seine. Churchill brings Peter Erwin back into the picture—solid, faithful Peter whom she should have married in the first place. Honora sees it all now; her purification is complete; she has learned her lesson. Peter has achieved greatness by remaining in St. Louis and following duty where it led. Great as he is, he qualifies in other respects that one is assured are of no importance now in Honora's mind but that nonetheless do no harm: he is famous and wealthy. Honora yields to his new proposal and agrees to another marriage, which one can imagine Churchill assumes will be a success but which may still leave some doubts in the minds of readers.

Churchill thought *A Modern Chronicle* was the best work he had yet done, but his immense reading public evidently did not agree with him. Sales did not quite match the mark set by previous Churchill novels.[4] Nevertheless, Grosset and Dunlap brought out a cheap edition of *A Modern Chronicle* in 1910 and again in 1914. Macmillan editions followed in 1920 and 1927. French and German editions were issued, although Churchill was said to have turned down an offer for a Swedish translation.

In general, although there was a slight fall-off in public interest in the novel, the critics agreed with Churchill that it was his best work. The *Nation* noted that *Mr. Crewe's Career* was an advance over his earlier novels: "In *A Modern Chronicle* a still further development is apparent."[5] The *Outlook* concurred when it said, "There is none of Mr. Winston Churchill's novels more carefully written or more thoroughly thought out than *A Modern Chronicle*," and added that the book presented "a composite portrait of American society."[6] William Morton Payne, who had reviewed many of Churchill's books in the *Dial*, said, "Mr. Churchill seems to have acquired a closer hold upon life than his romantic excursions have heretofore evidenced, and he has also improved in his literary technique."[7] Jeannette L. Gilder in *Bookman* was reminded of Edith Wharton's *House of Mirth*, though she did not find Honora Leffingwell as appealing as Mrs. Wharton's heroine. She thought the story was well worked out and recognized that many readers would consider it the author's best. "It is very true to certain phases of life as lived in America today, unfortunately too true."[8]

It is not difficult to agree with this contemporary critical opinion that *A Modern Chronicle* was a distinct advance in Churchill's art of fiction writing. Structurally, the novel is as nearly perfect as anything he ever did. Like *Coniston*, it lacks the diffuseness of so much of his other work and holds together well as a unified story. The plot revolves very naturally around Honora Leffingwell and the various types she meets. The pictures of Honora's early years in St. Louis, partly drawn perhaps from Churchill's own experience; the satirical portrait of high society, reminiscent of *The Celebrity*; the damning picture of suburbia dominated by the business mania—all are neatly, deftly drawn. The characters themselves are well done, except for Chiltern and Erwin.

The book represented the first attempt by Churchill to make a woman the central figure in the story, since Cynthia Wetherell in *Coniston* is subsidiary to Jethro Bass. Many critics had previously commented on the author's seeming inability to create female characters. Honora Leffingwell is the most convincing woman Churchill ever drew. To be sure, she has her contradictions; she learns to condemn the practices of Howard Spence but is quite willing to use the money that results from them. Churchill's predilection for seeing true heroes and heroines only in the genteel groups of the upper-middle classes forces him to give them sufficient means to maintain their station. Yet, at the same time, they invariably come to reject the traditional ways of making money and turn their backs on the world of business. Somehow or other, to be ideal men and women they must develop a contempt for high finance.

In the case of Honora Leffingwell, there is justification for the conflict she goes through. Churchill clearly implies that heredity was much to blame for her short-sighted, ambitious pursuit of happiness. At the same time, her St. Louis upbringing in the home of Tom and Mary Leffingwell left a puritanical impression on her mind, from which she both revolted and profited. On occasion, she could fall back on the older code, as she did in her affair with Trixy Brent. Honora is therefore a convincing portrait of contradictory tensions and emotions. She is a woman of force and of weakness; of modern ways and old-fashioned upbringing; of considerable refinement and poise and much passion. Above all, she is a woman with whom the reader sympathizes. Significantly, in pointing out the effects of Honora's heredity and environment on her character and personality, Churchill was employing a mild naturalism for the first time. Honora's desire to escape a humdrum life is vaguely similar to the impulses that move Dreiser's Carrie Meeber.

The weaknesses of the novel lie in the drawing of Peter Erwin and the inevitable happy ending. Erwin is too good; one wishes this pasteboard image of perfection were not even in the story. The ending, too, is a disappointment. How much more realistic and satisfactory from the standpoint of a modern reader would it have been to leave Honora at the end of her second marriage slowly awakening to the futility of her life and her mad pursuit of happiness. It would have been more tragic; and the story Churchill told in three-fourths of the book was essentially tragedy. He damages it all by thrusting in the concocted ending to lift Honora out of her misery and into a more satisfactory situation. It is a solution more suited to the comedy of manners than to the serious study Churchill was attempting.

It is customary to speak of *A Modern Chronicle* as a novel of divorce because there is little about the way divorces are obtained that Churchill does not tell. Honora's six-month Western divorce may be taken as a reflection on the reputation of such a place as Reno, Nevada. Although he clearly shows the effects of society's ostracism on the divorcée, some critics thought he was exaggerating this element, that no such exclusion existed in 1910. Churchill may have overdrawn the situation, for he was concerned about the rising divorce rate and about the breaking up of modern marriages, which he thought was too often due to preoccupations that assumed a greater importance in two lives than they should. At one point in the novel, he questions whether domestic happiness will survive the strains of the twentieth century.[9]

The novel is equally a damnation of Churchill's new villain, the selfish businessman and his unethical ways. The breakdown of Honora's first marriage is caused as much by Howard Spence's preoccupation with business—dishonest business, at that—as it is by Honora's boredom. And the preoccupation with business comes because in American society the male must scramble in the economic jungle to get ahead of his neighbor, to keep up materially with his class, or to advance to a new role, to make a good "deal" before someone else beats him to it. Perhaps Honora would not have been so bored if Howard had paid more attention to her and less to the stock market. American men believe that "a wedding-ring absolves them forever from any effort on their part to retain their wives' affections."[10] True to Thorstein Veblen's theory, the wife is to be kept at home for display—as one of the trophies of the economic law of "survival of the fittest." Certainly, Churchill suggests that in 1910 it was rare for a man to be as solicitous about his wife as he was about his business.

That Churchill continued to view modern marriage as one of the casualties of modern business is indicated by his succeeding novels in which he touched on the divorce theme again. Furthermore, he stated in a short essay for *Hearst's* of June, 1912, that he had given the divorce question much thought in the past few years and had about come to the conclusion that the problem would have to be left to the conscience of the individual, since "the day of external authority is rapidly passing."[11]

One year later, in July, 1913, Churchill elaborated on his earlier notions in more detail. In an article called "Our 'Common Sense' Marriages," prepared for *Good Housekeeping*, he said modern unions were not true marriages but business partnerships. The preoccupation of men with the "common sense" Adam Smith approach to life caused them to give their entire attention to business and financial interests. Women's ambitions, on the other hand, were governed by "the spectacle of what is called Society."[12] A clever husband made money; a clever wife advanced in the social world to further her husband's contacts so he could make more money. With such a vicious circle, Churchill stated, it was no wonder that American life was plagued with so many unhappy marriages, so many free and easy divorces.

By the time Churchill penned the *Good Housekeeping* article, he had written *The Inside of the Cup* and had voiced his strong social gospel notions. His answer, therefore, was an appeal to a true Christian approach to marriage; the Christian objective of service must be the core of wedlock. Moreover, "We have actually to make the choice between Christ and Adam Smith, and stick to one or the other."[13] The disappearance of the real Christian viewpoint toward life (not necessarily the church's viewpoint, by any means) was the cause of the disintegration of the family.

Churchill was also concerned with the subject of divorce in *The Inside of the Cup*. In his last two novels he touched on the issue, but in them he was more preoccupied with other cogent social questions. *A Modern Chronicle* remains as his major contribution to the subject of American marriage and its attendant problems. It is a pity that the theme of the book is now more or less outdated. Divorce novels, although not unknown today, scarcely stand on their own merits. Other issues must be present to force a conflict, since present-day ideas of divorce practices have altered so drastically. If the significance of divorce as an issue in American civilization were as challenging today as it was in 1910, *A Modern Chronicle* would be one of Churchill's better-known books, rivaling his historical romances in popularity. As it is, although Grant Knight has called it "one of the best novels of the last half of the decade" in which it was written, it is scarcely known to either modern readers or literary historians.[14] It deserves a better fate.

One final note indicates its further use for a student of American thought. In discussing the problems of divorce and modern marriage and in condemning, at least by strong implication, the prevailing laxness in divorce laws, Churchill was again in tune with the thought of Theodore Roosevelt. And in mentioning the reluctance of modern women to have large families, he was pursuing one of the favorite themes of the former President. Roosevelt's statements, sometimes amounting to diatribes, against birth control and the failure of the Anglo-Saxon race to reproduce itself are well-known.[15] There is no indication that *A Modern Chronicle* was directly inspired by Roosevelt's beliefs, but he must have found the book congenial to his thinking.

CHAPTER 5

In the Pulpit: the Social
Gospel Novel

I

IT WAS NOT UNNATURAL that Winston Churchill should have been concerned with religious matters and with the church's role in contemporary life as he turned his attention increasingly to current social and economic problems. There was much in his own background to suggest a religious turn of mind. His New England heritage, a conscious factor in much of his thought, included descent from Jonathan Edwards. For years he was an active communicant of the Protestant Episcopal Church. After he moved to New Hampshire, he was a supporter successively of St. Paul's Church in Windsor, Vermont, and of Trinity Church in Cornish. At various times he served as warden, lay reader, and vestryman for one or the other of these parishes. He was also very much interested in local Young Men's Christian Association work and frequently gave time, talent, and money to the Sullivan County, New Hampshire, unit. Whenever his heavy schedule would allow him to speak for such local or national groups, he did so. Frequently on these occasions he combined his religious remarks with exhortations for clean politics. In his campaign of 1906, he had appealed strongly to religious groups in focusing attention on the need for Christian principles in politics.

Churchill was also driven toward social gospel concepts by the thinking of his time. There was about the whole Progressive movement, both pre-1908 and post-1908, a religious tone that is difficult to match in the history of American political thought after the theocratic doctrines of the Puritans of the seventeenth century. The campaign of 1912 was conducted with all the frenzy of a revival meeting, for the Progressives were convinced that they were fighting for the true Christianity. Ralph Gabriel has said that "the social gospel was the religious phase of the progressive movement."[1] In the period from 1908 to 1912, the social gospel was especially strong in Progressive thought, but it was never absent during the entire span of Progressivism's existence on the political scene.

Even before he finished *A Modern Chronicle*, Churchill had contemplated the growing religious issues of the day. He himself had experienced some doubts about certain of his own church's doctrines, and he was fond of discussing these questions with his clergymen friends.[2] He also set about reading the comments of others on religious matters amidst the plethora of material that was available on the subject between 1910 and 1912. *Robert Elsmere*, Mrs. Humphrey Ward's popular religious novel of 1888, was still discussed. *In His Steps*, the best-seller of 1897, continued to be a popular favorite. The Reverend Harold Bell Wright was able to retire from the ministry to devote himself to writing after publishing *The Shepherd of the Hills*, a novel with religious overtones. Numerous magazine articles pointed to the current "spiritual unrest." Frank L. Mott has reported a new ten-cent series in 1910 that included Dr. Sheldon's *In His Steps*, Reverend Dwight L. Moody's *What Is Christ?*, Reverend C. H. Spurgeon's *John Ploughman's Talk*, Reverend C. W. Gordon's *Black Rock*, and others.[3] On a higher intellectual level, Walter Rauschenbush published his *Christianity and the Social Crisis* (1907), *Prayers of the Social Gospel* (1909), and *Christianizing the Social Order* (1912). The establishment of the Federal Council of Churches in 1908 was a further indication of the importance religion was assuming in the intellectual currents of the time. It was in this climate that Churchill did his reading and thinking of the "newer criticism."

Shortly after his return from abroad in the spring of 1910 and less than two months after publication of *A Modern Chronicle*, Churchill was helping in a successful political campaign in New Hampshire that culminated in the election of an old associate, Robert Bass, as governor. As if to underline his belief that politics and religion ought to be closely allied, he was also preparing his next novel—a book that was to deal with his new religious thinking. A city-oriented story, it was to raise issues involving high church doctrine, business machinations, and the slums and poverty of the day.

To gain background for such a book, Churchill enlisted the aid of clergymen friends in his studies. His published writings indicate he became familiar with the ideas of William Ellery Channing, Phillips Brooks, Henri Bergson, Thomas Carlyle, and Matthew Arnold. Later, William James and Josiah Royce were to interest him. Seeking a rational approach to religion that opposed ultra-refined theological argumentation and championed the new scientific views, Churchill thoroughly immersed himself in social gospel literature and questions. Meanwhile, he had hit upon an appropriate title, *The Inside of the Cup*—a phrase drawn from one of the rebukes of Christ to the Pharisees.

In July, 1911, Churchill broke into his writing routine to address the Seabury Conference of the Episcopal Church at Cambridge, Massachusetts. This speech represented Churchill's first major religious utterance before a substantial church group; earlier appearances had been before local congregations. The Seabury address attracted favorable public attention when it was reported in the press of the East. If Churchill intended it as a trial balloon, the Cambridge talk must have encouraged him to proceed with the speculations he was indulging in his novel.

The novel was also preceded by an *Atlantic* magazine essay that Churchill published in January, 1912. Entitled "Modern Government and Christianity," the article dealt with his own personal religious beliefs and their connection with democratic government. He thought he had found the key to world history in the development of greater and greater individual freedom. This, in turn, he felt was the true essence of Christianity—the substitution of individual autonomy for external authority, of genuine democracy for hierarchy and monarchy. Churchill saw in the revolt of Martin Luther the beginnings of modern learning and modern science. The Reformation also set in motion forces leading to changes in government. These changes had reached their culmination in the American Declaration of Independence. The system of universal suffrage was the application of the Christian principle of the worth of the individual, "the expression not only of an ideal but of a firm conviction that God resided in the soul of man, that the individual conscience was therefore the only authority for an enlightened people."[4] He went on to argue that true Christianity in the hearts of men would be manifested by less need for government. The simplicity of organization of the earliest Christian communities would become the symbolic model for modern government. Service would be the keynote of Christianity—not observance of a ritual or belief in mystic miracles. Service, of course, meant the social gospel. The spirit of Christ would be found in the struggle for economic and social reform.

In February, 1912, *Current Literature* summarized this *Atlantic* article under the heading, "Winston Churchill's Christian Anarchism."[5] The title was somewhat misleading, for Churchill did not go so far as to advocate anarchism of any kind. The title should have read "Winston Churchill's Christian Service," for service was a principle he was to stress over and over in his religious utterances until the end of his life. It was the one idea that did not change as his other religious notions did. It was first given expression in the *Atlantic* piece, but *Current Literature* scarcely noted it. The fact that *Current Literature* reviewed the essay, however, shows the impact his lectures and articles were beginning to have on the public mind. The growing significance of Churchill's influence is perhaps also illustrated by the placement of the Churchill essay between articles by William Graham Sumner and Ambassador James Bryce, followed by a discussion of Henri Bergson's philosophy. Churchill had arrived, at this point, in high intellectual company.

Meanwhile, as a speaker he was coming to the attention of religious groups. His well-known name and reputation were adequate assurances of an audience; furthermore, he was interested in the popular subject of social gospel reforms. Consequently, he was asked increasingly during 1911 and 1912 to voice his religious views before audiences. By the time his religious novel appeared, some of the public had already heard much of its message from the author's own lips.

Up to 1912, Churchill had serialized only one book, the first third of *The Crossing*. However, he was aware that magazine publication would greatly increase the circulation of the message he was currently eager to convey in his new book. When he received an offer from *Hearst's*, therefore, he decided to break precedent. Working with greater difficulty and intensity than ever before, he finished the novel in time for it to begin in the May, 1912, issue of the magazine. It ran in *Hearst's* for almost a year until April, 1913. Book publication by Macmillan came in March, 1913, just as the serial was nearing its last installment.

Churchill attempted in *The Inside of the Cup* to present his own personal working out of the problem of religion. He had no desire to speak as a would-be clergyman. However, the serialization of the story provoked so much comment, some of it ill-informed, that Churchill felt constrained to add an afterword to the book explaining that he had no desire to pose as a theologian and that he spoke for no one except himself.

The book, less a novel than a tract, concerns the Reverend John Hodder, who leaves a small church in the Northeast (probably in New England) to accept the call to St. John's in a large Mid-western city (probably St. Louis). Hodder, who had joined the ministry on the eve of becoming a successful lawyer, has orthodox views about Christianity. But an awakening starts with his intro-duction to the slums of the big city on the one hand, and to the high society of his new church on the other.

Hodder has been called to St. John's because it is assumed he would be "safe" in resisting the inroads of liberal social thought. One of his first encounters is with Eldon Parr, success-ful business man and millionaire leader of the church. Parr quickly informs Hodder of what is expected of him: orthodoxy in doctrine and conservatism in social theory. Above all, Parr says, St. John's will not tolerate socialists who call themselves ministers of God.

St. John's Church had originally been in a well-to-do section of town; but the city's growth has left it in a run-down slum area. Hodder is particularly impressed with the squalor and vice of nearby Dalton Street. At the same time, he sees that the church is serving only the wealthy, the socially élite who ride from distant homes to keep up their allegiance to the old parish. Hodder is grateful enough for this commuting support, but he wonders why the church does not reach the working men and women he sees all around him on the streets near St. John's. The Reverend Mr. McCrae, his assistant, says it is because the working men are no longer interested in religion.

Hodder then begins to learn that there are doctrinal doubts

in the minds of some of his wealthy parishioners. Eleanor
Goodrich comes to discuss with him the virgin birth, a belief she
finds quite outmoded and useless for the present age. Mrs.
Everett Constable asks him to marry her divorced daughter in
the church. When he refuses, her argument leaves him on pretty
hard and uncharitable grounds. Later, Eldon Parr's own daughter,
Alison, comes home from the East for a short visit. A charming,
talented girl, Alison meets Hodder and puts new doubts in his
mind. She has left home to seek her own way in the world
largely because she cannot support her own father's views.
She discusses with Hodder the condition of modern religion:
how the social system under modern industry is wholly un-
Christian, yet is endorsed by bulwarks of the church like her
father; how the clergy has lost its influence in contemporary
life because it has clung to orthodox religious ideas that cannot
stand under modern scientific inquiry; how the church's authority
has undermined rather than strengthened the faith of thinking
parishioners. She reveals a certain helplessness in coping with
all these paradoxes, but she cannot accept Hodder's orthodox
explanation. She tells Hodder she does not think he really
believes what he preaches. Gradually, he begins to question his
own pat answers when he finds he cannot solve the religious
riddles that Alison poses. She recommends that he consult the
"higher criticism" to find thinking that will be more congenial
with the contemporary age and that will answer the doubts
that are beginning to deluge his mind. When he follows the
suggestion, he learns that the works of men like William James
and Josiah Royce do truly substitute something more worth-
while for his earlier orthodoxy.

Simultaneously, Hodder finds out what kind of men his
wealthy parishioners really are. In a run-down tenement on
Dalton Street he meets a starving man who tells him the truth
about Eldon Parr. It is a story of a powerful businessman's
robbing the poor through the Consolidated Tractions Company
fraud; his thieving is within the law, but quite outside Christian
morality. And he is the same Eldon Parr who contributes to
charity and supports St. John's and its settlement house work.
Rector John Hodder readily sees the hypocrisy in Parr's philanthropic pose which is based, in truth, on a "system of legalized
or semi-legalized robbery and the distribution of largesse to

the victims."[6] In his walks along Dalton Street, Hodder also discovers a prostitute named Kate Marcy, once a fine girl who had loved Eldon Parr's son Preston. Parr had prevented the marriage because he felt Kate was not good enough for his son, had bought her off, and had thereby sent her, in her grief, into a life of sin.

These revelations result in the awakening of John Hodder. He decides during a summer vacation to remain at his post at St. John's and to work from within. But he will be a new pastor. He will blast the malpractices of the Parrs; he will attack a religion based wholly on autocracy and blind faith in mysteries; he will preach the true spirit of Christ as exemplified in service to mankind. He will, in short, preach the social gospel despite the problems he well knows this will raise with his congregation.

The reaction to the changed Hodder is not long in coming. Though a few are sympathetic, most of his parishioners are outraged by his new viewpoints. When, in effect, he asks them to choose between Christ or business, they choose business. A vestry meeting is called, over which Eldon Parr presides in all his financial might. He accuses Hodder of socialism—and insanity! He demands the rector's resignation or he will push with the bishop for a heresy trial. Hodder stands his ground; turmoil reigns in the church. But the poor hear the clergyman's message; they thrill at the gauntlet laid down to Eldon Parr and begin coming to services.

Meanwhile, Hodder and Alison Parr have fallen in love. This so infuriates Parr that he forbids the marriage, then announces he does not wish to see his daughter again and disinherits her when she refuses to obey him.

In a lengthy scene at the end of the book, Hodder accuses Parr of being an utter failure as a Christian. He charges that the plea "business is business" will not justify the deception, cheating, and stealing that often characterize the actions of trusted boards of directors in American enterprise; and he warns that an awakened public conscience, which is really the leaven of Christianity at work, will put a stop to such practices. Carrying his argument even further, he suggests that private property may eventually be abolished, since its possession gives the owner an un-Christian advantage over other people.[7] Parr, who thinks his charity will excuse him, mentions the sums he has given to libraries, to universities, to hospitals, and to churches as justification that the business practices of his age are for the benefit of society. Practical business is more charitable than impractical Utopia. But Hodder, who will not accept this as a true Christian viewpoint, maintains that effective Christian charity must come through larger cooperative groups—not through individuals.

At the end, Eldon Parr is a broken man. He loses his daughter to Hodder; he loses his son who dies of apoplexy and as an alcoholic because of his father's failure to sanction his marriage to Kate Marcy; worst of all, perhaps, he loses the battle for St. John's. Hodder, cleared by the old bishop, remains to make the church a new center of the social gospel, preaching a faith that the poor can adopt and urging true Christianity in a democratic economy.

The Inside of the Cup was the most controversial book Churchill ever wrote. The novel was immediately attacked by some ministers, rectors, and priests as an unjust picture of contemporary religion. More liberal clergymen, on the other hand, thought the book served as a needed warning for a house-cleaning in the church of both personnel and doctrine. Although Churchill had indicated no denomination in the novel, it seemed clear that he was speaking of his own church, the Episcopal. But his message applied to all denominations, Protestant and Catholic; and the clergy was quick to take the challenge. Laymen, too, read and discussed the book for the next few years. Public letters were exchanged about the merits of the ideas contained in the novel; sermons were preached about it. At least one pastor, the Reverend Henry R. Rose of the Church of the Redeemer in Newark, New Jersey, wrote and published a book in defense of Churchill's position. Titled "The Outside of the Cup: A Response to Winston Churchill's *The Inside of the Cup*," the text was actually a summation of eight sermons Rose had preached on the Churchill novel. Possibly no other work of fiction primarily concerned with religion and the church has created such a sensation as *The Inside of the Cup*. Only one other, Charles Sheldon's *In His Steps,* has superseded it in sales.

Certainly, the novel was a financial success. In spite of, or perhaps because of its controversial nature, the book went through more editions than any other Churchill novel after the historical romances. It was almost as if he had again captured the huge public audience he had held with *Richard Carvel* and *The Crisis*. American Macmillan had editions in 1913, 1914, 1918, 1921, and 1927. The book went into foreign translations, as well as English, Canadian, and Australian editions. Grosset and Dunlap brought out cheap reprints in 1913, 1915, and 1922. It was first on the *Bookman* best-seller list in 1913, third in 1914.[8] Ten years after its first publication it was still popular enough to be made into a silent movie by Paramount Films.

Because of the appeal of the subject and the solution to the religious questions of the day, the public found the novel stimulating and useful. The critics, however, were almost universally annoyed with its didacticism and its strong resemblance to a theological leaflet. The *Nation* thought the Reverend Hodder was the most unreal of any of Churchill's characters: "From first to last he is always preaching or preached to. Consequently, the story fails to move of itself, fails to be a story of persons and events."[9] William M. Payne in the *Dial* found the book too intensely serious: "The charge lies fairly against it that the author is so weighed down with the sense of his mission and so zealous in the bearing of his testimony that he neglects art for the sake of didacticism."[10] The *Catholic World* admitted, "We took up Mr. Churchill's book to be entertained, but we must confess we were bored instead."[11] Admiral Alfred T. Mahan, who might have been expected to have a natural sympathy for Churchill, wrote for the *Churchman* a diatribe against *The Inside of the Cup*; he called it a "caricature of the inner spirit of Christianity."[12] In London, the *Athenaeum* feared readers would become bored with so much theology, and the *Spectator* noted the total lack of comic relief.[13]

Many reviewers, however, commended Churchill for tackling the theme of religion; while deploring his art, they endorsed his moral earnestness and zeal. Such critics, of course, were quite correct in noting the author's seriousness. Starting with the historical romances, he had increasingly used his pen to educate the public. The problem novels were even more didactic. As he grew more earnest, he had to abandon true fiction and turn to the essay, either directly or in the disguised form of the propaganda novel. From *A Modern Chronicle* on, Churchill preached in the freest sense. *The Inside of the Cup* is merely the most obvious example of this.

At the same time, this commendable moral earnestness which led to sermonizing was partly responsible for Churchill's downfall as a popular novelist. It impeded his talents in the realm of fictional art. The characters in *The Inside of the Cup* are little more than vehicles for debate. The speech is often stilted and unnatural; and, although Churchill seldom wrote excellent dialogue except in *Coniston,* this novel has the worst in all his fiction. Of plot there is precious little. If the book bears any resemblance to fiction, it is in the psychological study of Hodder's awakening —a genuine fictional device. For the rest, the book should have been written as nonfiction. Indeed, it almost was, for whole chapters are given over to nothing but doctrinal debate and pulpit sermons.

But what of the ideas? These were important to Churchill; he was so intensely concerned with Christianity in democracy and with the gospel of service that he may have hoped to preach a message more than to entertain the public. If this was his aim, he succeeded admirably. Published at the height of the Progressive Party furore, *The Inside of the Cup* illustrated and increased the general religious tone of the cause. Its publication in *Hearst's* during the summer of 1912 undoubtedly helped Churchill capture the national eye and catapult his New Hampshire campaign. There is every indication that the book had great appeal to progressively inclined people.

As for the general public, it undoubtedly found Churchill's solution the best that had been offered since Edward Bellamy's *Looking Backward.*[14] For years, Churchill had appealed to middle- and upper middle-class taste. Not thorough intellectuals themselves, these people nevertheless liked to toy with pseudo-intellectual ideas; and that is about what *The Inside of the Cup* gave them opportunity to do. The Churchill solution was moral and it was safe. It was worked out *within* the confines of the church; it was important that Hodder did not break with his denomination. Later, Churchill was to abandon this notion, but at this time he held the more popular view of working from within to cleanse. The cleansing itself was not radical, for Gladden, Bliss, Herron, Rauschenbusch, Sheldon, and others had voiced very much the same idea before Churchill. By 1913, no one found it very upsetting. As the reviewer in the *Atlantic* put it, "What Winston Churchill has done for the readers of *The Inside of the Cup* is to give them his own theology as he has hewed it out of life. The greater part of it is your theology and mine. . . . We who are no longer young agree with him that there will be no socialistic society until all men are vitally Christian, and that, when this comes to pass, any form of society will be quite good enough."[15]

The book was not politically socialistic, despite first impressions that it might seem to be. The answer was strongly Progressive: work through the spirit of Christian brotherhood to achieve a life of service; the life of service would be most directly felt in social and economic reforms at the governmental level; liberal Christianity and democracy were one. Hodder found the secret to his religion in a sentence of Josiah Royce: "For your cause can only be revealed to you through some presence that first teaches you to love the unity of the spiritual life. . . . You must find it in human shape."[16] The human shape in *The Inside of the Cup* is Horace Bentley, the living incarnation of the true Christian spirit and a man who reminds one of Calvin Brinsmade in *The Crisis*. He is beloved of all and spends a devoted life in aiding the poor and comforting the sick. And he does this by serving them financially or in any way open to him—but not by preaching of the necessity of their enduring adversity to make their spirits strong. He no longer attends St. John's Church, but he is so much more a Christian than Eldon Parr that the contrast is almost embarrassing.

Despite the controversy *The Inside of the Cup* stirred in ministerial circles, Churchill's approach to his religion was acceptable, then, to a large American reading public because it was a midde-of-the-road position. He did not take the extreme view of the agnostics and the Socialists on the one hand or of the great body of conservatives and stand-patters on the other. He recognized that change was necessary; he saw that the old orthodoxy must bend. But in attacking some of the church's mysteries and in advising against a literal interpretation of biblical doctrines, he was urging a new church tie based on what he thought were infinitely stronger links. And in denouncing materialism and selfish business enterprise, he did not turn to Socialism as such as a solution, but to the Christian spirit of true brotherhood. What Churchill had really said was that the church must be converted from an organized hypocrisy into an active agency for social welfare, and its inner motive of action must become an unshaken conviction that the essence of Christianity is the realization of human brotherhood rather than belief in any miracle or lip-service to any creed. If this seems a naïve failure to dig to the root of the economic and social problems of his day, one should consider how much the message might apply to our own time. The question of modernism versus orthodoxy has not yet been settled and some of the business issues raised in the novel have not been quieted. One can still find some individual churches that are controlled largely by the business proclivities of the principal economic supports in the congregation.[17] Clearly, *The Inside of the Cup* is not altogether a book of its time; its message still has some application today.

Since *The Inside of the Cup* was one of the two most popular social-gospel novels written by Americans and one of the three most popular read by Americans, it invites comparison with its rivals, Mrs. Humphrey Ward's *Robert Elsmere* (1888) and Charles Sheldon's *In His Steps* (1897), also best-sellers of their day. All three books were on similar subjects: changing the emphasis in the religion of their times from forms and supernaturalism to Christian ethics and social reform. All served as conversation pieces in the pulpit, the home, and on the streets, but *In His Steps* had less controversial material in it than either *Robert Elsmere* or *The Inside of the Cup*. However, *The Inside of the Cup* exhibits two basic differences that mark the shift in religious thought between 1888-97 and 1912-13. First, the lapse of time made it possible for Churchill to be more hopeful about his ultimate solution than either Mrs. Ward or Sheldon had been. The book ends on a note of optimism that, false though it may be, reveals something of the Progressive reforms already made in the intervening time. And, second, the argument in Churchill's book has noticeably shifted. It is no longer based on dogmatic theology, but on the church as a social agency, upon its practical rather than its purely intellectual shortcomings.

These differences mark Churchill clearly as the child of his age—an age in which social sympathy had been aroused as never before. It is noteworthy that in the election of 1912 all political parties—Republican, Democrat, and Progressive—claimed the mantle of "progressive." No one dared stand against the tide, at least publicly. And though the Progressives themselves lost as a party, the reform measures many of them advocated were swept into being through the election of Woodrow Wilson. The social sympathy of *The Inside of the Cup* was indicative of the prevailing national mood.

II

Churchill did not cease his religious disputations with *The Inside of the Cup*. Shortly after the failure of the Progressive campaign in November, 1912, the Churchills journeyed to California where they took up temporary residence in Berkeley near the campuses of the University of California and the Pacific Theological Seminary. The trip seems to have been motivated at least partly by Churchill's desire to discuss the new questions of religion and psychology with some of the professors at the two institutions.

It was at this time that Churchill may have actually thought of the notion of going into the pulpit officially as a clergyman.[18] During 1913 he preached a number of lay sermons in Episcopal churches on the Pacific Coast, and in the summer of that year he interrupted his studies and his writing to deliver a series of religious lectures in the East. In the fall and winter of 1913-14 he occasionally discussed his new notions of social Christianity before groups at the University of California, and he continued to speak from the pulpits of the West Coast.

In December, 1913, *Century* magazine published one of these addresses given before "one of the most conservative Protestant Episcopal churches of the Pacific Coast, where it instantly attracted widespread attention."[19] Entitled "The Modern Quest for a Religion," the article is noteworthy for the New Patriotism he was now preaching. Based on social righteousness, the New Patriotism consisted of five tenets. First, it meant a change from the motive of the old acquisition of property to the new one of service to mankind. Second, it proclaimed a militant righteousness, a willingness to acknowledge and grapple with the problem of evil. Third, it was characterized by open-mindedness and an eagerness to change through growth. Fourth, the New Patriotism recognized the worth and dignity of every individual, regardless of his social station. This principle led to individual responsibility and to true democracy through universal suffrage. Finally, it emphasized the spiritual as well as the material needs of man. Culture, as well as food, warmth, and material luxuries, must be extended to all mankind.

Churchill readily acknowledged the skepticism, the "divine discontent" of his times, the search of men for a genuine religion. He felt the New Patriotism must serve as the basis for any such new reinterpretation of faith. Actually, what he was advocating was nothing except a code of ethics that had long been suggested by his predecessors in the path of Christian Socialism. There was also a groping for some individual identification with the personality of Christ that harks back to transcendentalism.[20] Churchill may not have realized his debt to the Neoplatonic aspects of transcendentalism, for he arrived at his conclusions after studying pragmatism, and he thought of his solution as modern insofar as pragmatism was modern. But pragmatism had sprung, too, of course, from the idealistic optimism of the Emersonian era.

As Churchill delved into economic issues for his next novel, *A Far Country*, he continued to voice his thoughts on religion. After he returned to the East in 1914 he lectured before college and seminary groups. Contemporary news accounts indicate that two years later he was still on the religious circuit. In 1917, he was closely enough identified with the church to write a short story for the Episcopal Pension Fund. Called "The Faith of Frances Craniford," the story illustrated how the church neglected its clergymen and their widows, particularly those in out-of-the-way parishes or in mission posts. It was published by the Episcopal Church in an effort to increase contributions to its clergymen's pension fund. Indeed, until World War I hushed the controversy over religion and grasped Churchill's own attention, religion was one of the two predominant subjects in his thinking. And once the war was over, it became the dominant thought until the end of his life. His religious views altered considerably, as the story of his last years shows; but his interest in theology and religion was the one that stayed with him the longest and the one he bore until his dying day.

A modern reader may be tempted to doubt the significance of many of Churchill's religious answers of these years. Though *The Inside of the Cup* treats some still unsolved problems, it seems on the whole too superficial today; the religious articles lack the perceptive depth that further discussion lent to the same ideas after the Progressive era. At the time, Churchill did not clearly understand the issues behind the wrongs he had cited; if he had, he could not have offered such patently simple solutions and been so optimistic about their success. He himself later repudiated some of the book's tenets. But in 1912 and 1913 Churchill's published thoughts were of great significance to the millions who read and discussed them. Readers took their Churchill seriously; hence, he is a seismograph of the popular temper.

Churchill did not care for the Darwinian theories of laissez-faire and unbridled competition in a materialistic America; but, instead of coping with them directly as a later generation had to do, he took the typically Progressive road of high-sounding morality and individual regeneration. Truth and goodness were positive, identifiable things; falsehood and evil were also easily marked. Like Roosevelt, his mentor, he was out of step with the true intellectual prophets—the minority of his time—men like Lippmann, Bourne, Laski, and Brooks; but Churchill was impressively in step with the overwhelming bulk of the American people who clung to the old truths about politics and morals. Controversial as his ideas might be, they were not something that was anathema, like those of the Socialists or of the International Workers of the World. Though there were some curious charges of socialism made against Churchill that he could never understand, the majority of Americans considered him safe enough. They found him stimulating and worth-while because he challenged the prevailing economic winds but did not offer any radical, dangerous alternatives. To read him was to salve the conscience, but not to upset society. Small wonder it is, then, that he stood at the head of the best-seller lists with *The Inside of the Cup*.

CHAPTER 6

Economic Issues: the Later
Problem Novels

I

POLITICS, modern marriage, and the Church had now been investigated and discussed at some length in Churchill's novels. One other large area of Progressive concern remained. Between 1910 and 1917, labor problems and the social unrest resulting from the development of modern industry proved to be two of the most popular subjects for fiction writers. Theodore Dreiser, Booth Tarkington, Sherwood Anderson, Jack London, David Graham Phillips, Robert Herrick, Ernest Poole, and Upton Sinclair were among those who exploited economic issues in their fiction during these years; and Churchill, too, was preparing to deal with economics more directly than he had in *A Modern Chronicle* or in *The Inside of the Cup*.

Soon after the fall election of 1912, he set to work on a new novel. The removal of the Churchill family to Berkeley, California, gave the author opportunity not only to discuss some of the issues of modern religion and psychology with the University of California professors but also to initiate some reading in the realm of economics—a field that he felt should be associated with religious principles since he now believed that true religion meant a life dedicated to service rather than to the profit motive. Such Progressive texts as Walter Weyl's *The New Democracy*, Bruce Wyman's *Control of the Market,* and Fabian Ware's *The Worker and His World* were available for his sampling as well as representative works from the Manchester school of economics. Upton Sinclair called his attention to tracts and writings in the field of syndicalism and socialism.

It is likely that when Churchill met Jack London he was again exposed to socialist doctrine. From 1914 on, he kept abreast of issues in *The New Republic,* the magazine founded by his Cornish neighbor, Herbert Croly. Many years later Churchill was to report that he was "affected by the doctrines of social reform which were in the air at the time and which were urged . . . by Mr. H. G. Wells."[1] In customary fashion, he chose to achieve familiarity with his source materials before writing economic fiction.

By the fall of 1914, the Churchills were back in New England, spending about as much time in Boston as at Cornish. By this time, too, the author's first investigation into the field of economic relations and modern industrial problems was completed. Taking his cue from the biblical story of the prodigal son, Churchill entitled the book *A Far Country.* Following the precedent set by *The Inside of the Cup,* he sold the serial rights to *Hearst's International Magazine. Hearst's* started the story in March, 1914, by advertising that it was a big thrust at lawyers and legislators; the magazine further recommended that people read the "great novel or else argue themselves out of date."[2] Book publication did not come until over a year later in June, 1915. It was reprinted twice that same month, along with Canadian and English editions, but serial publication had evidently hurt book sales. Another American Macmillan edition was not necessary before 1922; a third and final one was included in the Uniform Edition of 1927—three editions in all, not many for a Churchill novel. Clearly, it proved to be less popular than *The Inside of the Cup;* and it in no way matched the sales of the historical romances or of the political novels. However, one must remember that thousands who read the story in serialization did not bother to buy the book.

A Far Country must have pleased the Progressive mind, for it appeared before the ferment had died out. American scholars and liberals associated with the Progressive Party movement were taking a keen interest in the welfare of the common man. The thesis of Churchill's novel was one dear to the hearts of such liberals, namely, the damnation of laissez faire economics, an indictment of corporation practices in modern government, and a clear implication of regulation of big business. Both Roosevelt and Wilson Progressives could agree on regulation—

regulation of monopoly, as far as the Rooseveltians were concerned; regulation of competition for the Wilsonites. Like the prodigal son, Churchill was saying, America had strayed from the idealistic homeland of the fathers but would finally return to the forefathers' house, educated and matured by its excursion into the materialism of the profit motive.

Churchill returns in this novel to the autobiographical method of *Richard Carvel* and *The Crossing*. Hugh Paret, a corporation lawyer, tells his story in the first person as he reflects in late years on the factors that led him to stray into the path of the prodigal. Hugh regards himself as a typical American in the sense that his story is that of the usual seeker after material wants and desires. The acquisitive character that he developed, Hugh says, was a trait that the educational system of the 1870's and 1880's indirectly promoted. The achievement of his goals brought both success and disillusionment.

Brought up in a city that closely resembles Pittsburgh, Hugh grows to maturity in the post-Civil War era of industrial expansion and quick fortunes. His father is a lawyer of high principles who adheres to the older Calvinist code, and the youth quickly learns to fear him at the same time that he holds him in respect. Hugh learns to dissimulate early in life in order to circumvent his practical-minded father who has small use for the idealistic daydreams of the son. Churchill dwells at some length on Hugh's upbringing, his early adventures in the city, and his early flirtations. He is obviously concerned with heredity as a factor in his hero's development, another indication perhaps that Churchill was groping for Dreiseresque or naturalistic devices in his latest fiction.

Hugh begins his journey into the "far country" when he determines to go to college, not for an education but to prove to his friends that he is as capable as they. He has been dismayed and embarrassed by his father's plan to send him into his uncle's business after his graduation from high school, for his friends are going on to such places as Harvard, Yale, and Princeton. After a short apprenticeship in the affairs of the wholesale grocery house, he goes to night school and prepares to pass examinations for Harvard. When he is successful and gains admission, he tells his father of his intention, and Paret Senior gives him a belated blessing.

Hugh enters Harvard in 1881, where he quickly learns that the right contacts and friendships are more important than classroom work. After a brief idealistic encounter with an English teacher, Alonzo Cheyne, who advises him that he has marked talents in the field of writing, he seeks more materialistically rewarding acquaintances. Hugh cultivates the liking of the dilletantish and wealthy sons of the world of business and finance; and he scorns the proffered friendship of Hermann Krebs, the idealistic but poor son of a German immigrant, who has come to Harvard for serious study.

During a vacation interlude at the home of his wealthy friend, Jerry Kyme, Hugh makes the acquaintance of Theodore Watling, a corporation lawyer from his home city. Watling's power, importance, and influence are quickly made clear to him; Watling is listened to, his advice is heeded, he is a man who counts. The impression on the young student is conclusive. Hugh resolves that this is the type of person he wishes to be.

Fired now by his zest to succeed, Hugh soon enters Harvard Law School where he is taught not only the importance of his profession, but also the obligation to preserve, untrammeled and unchanged, the sacrosanct federal constitution. His graduation brings him back home where he soon comes to the attention of Theodore Watling. Watling, who has taken a liking to Hugh, apparently recognizes in him a lad with a drive for power, and he invites the young Harvard graduate to join his legal firm. This marks the beginning of Hugh's apprenticeship to the ways of the older man—ways devious but effective.

Hugh is quick to learn. Impressed always with the power and authority of the big business leaders with whom he works, he quickly sees that they are the true rulers of government, not the political hacks who are merely fronts to do their bidding. Hugh's circle of friends includes Miller Gorse, attorney for the leading railroad of the state; Adolf Scherer of the Boyne Iron Works; Leonard Dickinson of the Corn National Bank; Frederick Grierson, a wealthy real-estate man; Ralph Hambleton, a cynical friend of his youth who has become a leading financier; and Judah B. Tallant, owner of the corporation-controlled press. This set of businessmen rule their city and state, and Hugh quickly becomes one of their agents, for he recognizes that this is the means to success and power.

One of his first triumphs is in pushing House Bill No. 709 through the state legislature. This is a measure that, in a round-about way, makes it possible for monopolies to mushroom in general; more specifically, it enables the Boyne Iron Works to take over the Ribblevale Steel Company. In a capital that resembles Harrisburg, Hugh learns the machinations of railroad rule of the state. As in the political novels, Churchill drew on his own political experience for this chapter.

Later, Hugh argues a case that results in the reversal of a court judgment against the railroad—one that had awarded damages to a poor victim of an accident clearly caused by railroad negligence. (Again, Churchill was drawing on his New Hampshire experience.) Hugh assists in the "lateral expansion" of the Boyne Iron Works, Ltd., by drawing up documents that cleverly evade legal restrictions against monopolies. He joins in the Riverside franchise deal that brings a financial bonanza to his coterie of friends but a multitude of protests from the city's morally disturbed residents and the ruination of the plans of the city's Improvement League. Perhaps his greatest achievement is in creating a dummy company to bid for a telephone franchise in the city, enabling his own client, the Ashuela Telephone Company, to perpetuate its communications monopoly of the area. Everywhere private interest conflicts with public-spirited idealism—and everywhere idealism falls.

The climax of Hugh's meteoric rise in the world of corporations comes when he is summoned to New York to assist the most important financial leader of the nation, the great Personality, in devising schemes for getting around the Sherman Anti-trust Law. The Personality is clearly J. P. Morgan, and some of the material in the Morgan scenes was probably inspired by the Pujo Committee investigations of 1912-13. Hugh feels he has reached the pinnacle of success in being asked to serve as counselor for the Personality. It is something of anticlimax, therefore, when he is urged by the big business king-makers to be their candidate for the United States Senate to succeed his mentor, Theodore Watling, who has guarded the gates, first against the Populists and the agitators in Washington, and now against an obstreperous President (obviously Theodore Roosevelt) who somehow has slipped into office through an unpardonable blunder.

The story of Hugh's awakening from this notorious journey into the far country is the story of the Progressive ferment of the early 1900's. An aroused public begins to grow restless when the excesses of the business magnates are exposed. A Citizens' Union, led by many of Hugh's boyhood friends, is formed to wrest control of the city government from the boss, Judd Jason, and his superiors, the corporation-financial circles whom Hugh represents. Hermann Krebs, who has dogged Hugh's steps all the way from Harvard, sparks the movement that capitalizes on public indignation at the exposures a national muckraking magazine, *Yardley's Weekly,* has printed. A storm of civic righteousness has swept the city, as it has much of the rest of the nation; and the country seems destined finally to make a clean sweep of corporation control of government.

Tied in with this narrative of business manipulation of politics is the love story. In their youth, Hugh and Nancy Willett had loved each other, but Nancy turns from him as he changes during the Harvard years. Gradually, she becomes hardened by the world much as Hugh has, and finally she makes a marriage of convenience with Hambleton Durrett, a wealthy, dissolute playboy. In the meantime, failing to talk Nancy out of this union and into one with himself, Hugh meets and marries Maude Hutchins, a rather colorless woman who grows stronger in character as Hugh grows weaker. Three children are born, but Hugh is so busy with his career that he can find little time to spend with them or his wife. His idea of a good marriage is for the wife to remain at home as an adornment to her husband's success. Later on, Nancy and Hugh discover that they still love each other, and Hugh suggests an affair which Nancy sadly rejects. By this time, Maude has suspected things; taking the children, she leaves Hugh and goes to France to live until Hugh recovers his senses. Hugh has almost talked Nancy into getting a divorce when Durrett has an accident that leaves him incapacitated for life. Nancy feels she cannot leave Durrett now, and she rejects Hugh altogether. For the first time, Hugh has failed to get what he wanted.

Coupled with this private crisis is the stress and storm of the campaign against the Citizens' Union. At a crucial point, Hugh hears a speech by Krebs and finally capitulates to the reform point of view. He has been weakening for some time;

indeed, there have been moments throughout his life when he has had twinges of conscience. These finally get the better of him at the end of the book; he has a nervous breakdown and is forced to retire to California for recuperation. In the end, he rejects the way of the prodigal—the way of unbridled competition for the material rewards of life and, above all, the path of dishonest corporate rule. He decides to return to Maude and his children in France. Now his purpose is to devote his life to educating his children in the right paths that he had lost somewhere along the way.

The book is admittedly didactic, and the critics took Churchill to task for it: "Mr. Churchill has the lecture habit in an aggravated form, and it is seriously impairing his function as a novelist in any artistic sense. . . . He makes himself wearisome by excess of argument, and he distorts the facts of life by excess of emphasis."[3] "His real desire is not to be an entertainer, or even an artist; he aspires to become a lay preacher, even a minor prophet."[4] But once the didacticism and weak character portrayal were pointed out, many reviewers saw the book as another great Churchill achievement. Frederick Tabor Cooper in the *Bookman* thought Churchill had treated his theme better than Robert Herrick or David Graham Phillips had done.[5] His Americanism was praised by other reviewers who found his themes, as usual, the big issues confronting all America. "As a literary artist he may be said not to exist; as a voice on matters that are vitally important to us as Americans he is immensely important," asserted Hildegard Hawthorne in the New York *Times*.[6] In general, the critics tended to view *A Far Country* much less seriously as an artistic creation; but they still felt, like Miss Hawthorne, that Churchill was voicing important problems of the time. Whether they praised him or damned him depended upon whether they thought this function of literature was a legitimate one.

Some readers were beginning to suspect Churchill of radical sympathies. There are indications that he cared little for his popularity at this point; but, if Churchill had been carefully gauging it, he might have taken a cue from Theodore Roosevelt who wrote him his impressions of *A Far Country* in August, 1915. After stating that he was in general agreement with what Churchill had said in the book, Roosevelt implied that he hoped

the author was not going too far to the left: "Some time I hope
you will write a book which shall contain the complement of
your teaching. . . . The labor people are not one whit better
than the capitalists. The mass of them on one side is about like the
mass on the other; and while the very worst labor people are
no worse than the very worst among the capitalists, they so
completely outnumber them as to be on the whole as great an
element·of danger to the community."[7] This view was probably
shared by many of Churchill's middle-class readers, and it may
have accounted, in part, for his dwindling sales.

By all standards, *A Far Country* is a long book, too long even
for its day. Churchill, who spends too much time with Hugh's
youth, presents details that seem irrelevant and have no direct
bearing on the major portion of the story. He lessens the habit
of preaching only a trifle; there is still too much haranguing
and unnatural conversation. Like *The Inside of the Cup,* portions
of *A Far Country* should have been written as an essay. There
is also the usual weak character portrayal; Hugh Paret is too
wooden and his dialogue frequently resembles a dull sermon.
The minor figures, especially Theodore Watling and Hugh's
father, are better drawn than the protagonists, but none of them
is done with artistic touch. The plot is better than *The Inside
of the Cup,* although it still follows the romantic mold—with
one significant exception. Hugh does not get his first love, the
woman of his dreams; he has to be satisfied finally with his
mild attachment to his wife. The love scenes themselves are
almost curiosities; wholly passionless and bookish, they sound
as if Churchill were still a believer in several Victorian conven-
tions about sex.

A Far Country is interesting, however, because of the changing
point of view Churchill shows toward the social ills of America
and the political scene he knew. Although the older Progressive
emphasis on a moral solution is present and although there is
still talk of throwing the rascals out and of putting honest men in
government, Churchill now recognizes that this is not enough.
Something is wrong with the system; something deeper is at
fault in the social structure. Hermann Krebs, who undoubtedly
speaks for Churchill on many occasions, is fond of remarking
about the failure of the older reform sentiment based upon
morality and finally concludes that the talk of individual political

"wickedness" misses the main point of the corruption. Society itself, as presently constituted, is the principal cause of the current disorder. A better democracy must await a reorganization of social patterns.

This sentiment reflects the change in Progressivism. This is the newer thinking of the 1912 era, no longer the exclusive reliance on an awakened moral fervor, but a recognition that deeper reforms are necessary, that the very structure of society may have to be changed. Sometimes, Churchill seems to skirt close to socialism as an answer to the nation's problems. In *A Far Country* he shows sympathy for the organized labor movement as such for the first time. Krebs, the hero of the book in one sense, is the champion of labor; and whenever working men are depicted in the novel, they are shown in a favorable light.

Yet, the panacea that Churchill was groping for was not socialism in the accepted sense. It was not the socialism of an obscure political party, nor was it the brand then advocated by Christian Socialists. When Hugh asks Krebs to define his type of socialism, Krebs replies that it is the principles of rational religion and modern science applied to government. It was this synthesizing of science, government, and religion that Churchill saw as a solution. The argument was cloudy, since it was not yet clear in his own mind; but he seemed to feel that by accepting a Darwinian concept of religion and by applying the rules of biology to society an evolution would take place socially and politically that would bring about true democracy.

The parable of the prodigal son is the parable of democracy, Krebs says. In order to advance, America had to take its journey into the far country of unbridled individualism and materialism. Now, from this lesson, something better will evolve. Krebs suggests to Hugh that he acquaint himself with modern science, psychology and sociology, and that he try to understand the economic principles which lie behind the labor and the woman's rights movements. Using his reason, man can perfect his society, Krebs believes. As for religion, the church of the future will have a strong undergirding in the scientific point of view. In short, science now offers the solution to all things—political, social, and religious.

As far as Churchill was concerned, this notion probably represented the result of his studies in California. Nationally,

of course, it was a reflection of the change in Progressive sentiment, for the reliance on science was something shared by nearly
all Progressives after the 1908 era. It was another plank in the
gospel of progress, and Churchill again showed his identification
with Progressivism's cause by espousing it in his latest novel.

II

Despite its length, *A Far Country* represented only part of
Churchill's exposition of the industrial problem. He had more
that he wanted to say about the chaotic conditions brought
about by the rise of big business. Specifically, he wished to
discuss labor issues in more detail. Whether Churchill was
impelled by the general public interest in labor matters that
developed just before World War I is difficult to say. If such
public preference was a factor in his thinking, it only furthered
his own inclination toward the subject. Both *The Inside of the
Cup* and *A Far Country* had suggested labor themes. The condition of the workers in the factories of the new era had been
a consideration of his reforming zeal for some time. Furthermore,
his return to Boston in the fall of 1914 gave him opportunity
to study a recent labor struggle that could be examined at
first hand.

Churchill decided to focus his next novel on the activities
of the Industrial Workers of the World at nearby Lawrence,
Massachusetts. A prolonged strike of weavers in the textile mills
there in 1912 had resulted in victory for the labor forces. This
strike, together with the Paterson silk strike a year later, brought
the Industrial Workers of the World—the "Wobblies"—to the
East. Organized in Chicago in 1905 but confined largely to the
Pacific Northwest, the Industrial Workers had encountered
little success in spreading beyond that region until the Lawrence
strike brought them to the favorable attention of laboring groups
over the entire nation. Later, during World War I and after,
the "Wobblies" were severely crippled and then smashed when
anti-syndicalist laws were passed by many states and the group's
leaders were jailed. In 1914 and 1915, however, the "Wobblies"
had captured national attention and some labor support. The
Lawrence agitation was therefore a timely example for Churchill
to study.

Supplementing his first-hand coverage of the locale of the strike, Churchill continued his reading—and, perhaps more important, his conversations with Progressive friends. During this period he knew Herbert Croly, Roscoe Pound, Louis Brandeis, Learned Hand, William McAdoo, Harold Ickes, Frank Knox, John C. Winant, and James Bryce—several of whom may have extended his own political thinking into the newer realms of economics and sociology.

Yet Churchill had a conservative balance to match all his liberal influences. Friends like George W. Vanderbilt and the relatives of the Edward H. Harriman family could scarcely have planted many radical notions in his mind. Despite his natural sympathy for the economic underdog, Churchill frequently traveled in the company of the wealthy social set. Withal, his own conservative background helped to balance the ultra-liberalism of some of his Progressive acquaintances.

The result was a more middle-of-the-road approach than some parts of the later novels might indicate. Churchill, in fact, is an excellent example of the typical Progressive who may have been scathing in his criticism of American society but was mild enough in the solution he proposed. Here again, the parallel with Theodore Roosevelt could be noted. Churchill's very sense of moderation, the need for striking the middle way between the ultra-liberals and the ultra-conservatives was nowhere more apparent than in his endorsement of Theodore Roosevelt, a mild patrician liberal, whose Progressivism stopped abruptly when it reached the end of a rather short tether.

Two magazine articles that Churchill wrote about this time further illustrate his moderate approach to issues. In the summer of 1916, he attended the Progressive Party convention—no longer as a delegate, but only as a spectator. Later, he wrote his impressions of the convention in a *Collier's* magazine piece called "Roosevelt and His Friends," an article strongly eulogistic of Roosevelt and showing that Churchill's Progressivism, for the moment at least, went only as far as the former President's.[8] A somewhat earlier article, an essay in *Harper's* for January, 1916, showed even more clearly how cautious Churchill's liberalism was. Indeed, it is difficult to explain this essay except as the "complement" to his teaching that Roosevelt had written him about in August, 1915, for it contradicted many of the tenets advanced in his two economic-problem novels.

Entitled "A Plea for the American Tradition," the article decried the "foreign" solutions that were being attempted to meet the perplexing problems of the new, complex industrial age. The author deplored strong government action that amounted to class legislation and argued that old-age pensions, minimum-wage laws, and workingmen's compensation acts might "be necessary to secure a temporary measure of justice, but fundamentally they are not American."[9] Harking back to the earlier phase of Progressivism, he urged that American traditions be studied and readopted as a solution for the nation's woes; and he reverted to the faith that the real American spirit could again be restored to men's hearts and to the belief that government's only function was to guarantee equality of opportunity to all. The fairly conservative article was certainly anti-Marxist, anti-class strife, and, in its overtones, antipathetic to foreign influences; by implication, it was chary of further immigration.

The *Harper's* essay is even more interesting because it appeared at the time Churchill was putting the finishing touches to his labor novel, a book that in some respects was to contradict the assumptions of the essay. The third successive book Churchill serialized, *The Dwelling-Place of Light* began running in *Hearst's International Magazine* during the summer of 1916. Macmillan's publication was in October, 1917, after the United States had entered the World War and after American interest had left the domestic scene for foreign fields. Partly because of this situation and partly because of serial publication, the novel was the least successful, in terms of sales, that Churchill ever published. There were cheap editions in 1917 and 1919, but Macmillan did not have another edition until the Uniform Edition of all of Churchill's works in 1927. Neither Mott nor Hart mentions the book in his discussion of best-sellers.[10] For the first time, a Churchill novel did not appear on the *Bookman* best-seller list as reported by Alice Hackett.[11] Churchill's reading public seemingly was deserting him, although, again, it is difficult to say how real this desertion was since many read the story not in book form but in the *Hearst's* magazine version.

The Dwelling-Place of Light was the second book in which Churchill told his story from a woman's point of view. In

A Modern Chronicle he had created his best female character in
Honora Leffingwell; in *The Dwelling-Place of Light* he did an
admirable, though less successful, portrait in Janet Bumpus.
Janet and her sister Lise are the daughters of Edward and
Hannah Bumpus, descendants of original Puritan settlers of
Massachusetts. Edward, the father, takes great pride in studying
his genealogy; it has, indeed, become his religion since the old
verities seem to have crumbled all about him. His social and
economic status has crumbled with them. By a process of erosion,
which Churchill says is characteristic of modern industrial
civilization, Bumpus finds himself reduced to the menial task of
gatekeeper for the Chippering Mill in Hampton. Unlike his
illustrious ancestors, he lives near the bottom of the economic
bracket in a tenement area bordering on the slums. His only
claims to gentility are his continued interest in the family tree
and his Yankee aversion to the new hordes of immigrants. The
mother, Hannah, scoffs at her husband's interest in his ancestry
and blames their economic condition on Edward's inability to
push forward in the new world of unbridled competition.

Janet and Lise are forced to go to work at an early age. Lise,
the younger sister, is employed as a clerk in the Bagatelle, one
of the cheaper department stores of Hampton. Janet is a
stenographer in the office of the manager-agent of the Chippering Mill, Mr. Claude Ditmar. Neither girl is satisfied with her
work or with her station in life; both yearn for better things and
are impelled by an inward force to seek larger fields. Janet's
break comes when she draws the attention of her employer,
Claude Ditmar, a self-made business tycoon who has risen by
practising the survival-of-the-fittest doctrine. He notices one day
that Janet has a spark, a passion, that is different from the other
women of his acquaintance. A man of action, he suspects a new
field for conquest, and soon makes her his private secretary.

Janet is taken aback by Ditmar's advances, for she still retains
something of the older Puritan moral code in her fibre. But she
also yearns to be a free spirit; there is something within her
that makes a break with the past. Janet's search is for the
dwelling place of light—for some road to the achievement of
self-realization. As Ditmar pursues her, she rejects his advances,
at first because of the traditional moral code but later because
of the modern woman's sense of pride in her new-found

individuality and worth. She cannot make up her mind whether she loves Ditmar or not, though she feels passionately drawn to him. But she does realize that he offers her an avenue of escape.

At last, Janet succumbs when Ditmar finally offers marriage—albeit at some time in the future—at the same time that he intensifies his pursuit. On a Sunday in winter, she journeys with him to Boston where he has arranged for them to have dinner in a hotel room together. It is clear he has planned her seduction, though Churchill leads one to believe he is also very much in love with her. The trap is closed at the Sunday assignation, and Janet immediately recognizes that a great change has come over her life.

Meanwhile, Janet's sister Lise has also sought freedom from the boredom of her existence. Lise has fled to movies, cheap magazines, and dance halls for her release. Lacking Janet's finer sensitivity and her ideals, Lise moves from one male friend to another, relaxing her standards as she goes. On the very same Sunday that Janet and Ditmar journey to Boston, Lise, who has discovered she is going to have a baby, flees with her latest escort to the same city for an abortion. When Janet returns and learns of her sister's flight, she pursues her to the dingy house where the salesman-lover, a married man, has taken her. This shocks Janet into realizing that her own case is not so different from Lise's; she has followed Lise's course on a more sophisticated level. Both have been victims, however, of seduction. Later, when Lise discovers that she is not pregnant after all, she decides to continue on the more alluring primrose path rather than to return to the monotony of life in Hampton.

At this point the larger issues intrude. All along, Churchill has sketched the conditions of the workers in Ditmar's Chippering Mill and has given Janet glimpses of their sorry plight. Although Claude Ditmar is kind to his employees, he is adamant in his opposition to unions. He is also completely unconcerned about the living conditions of his laborers. When a reformer who has taken a survey of housing conditions in Hampton tries to interest Ditmar in improving the workers' home environment, Ditmar replies that the immigrants prefer to live as they do since they were used to such conditions in Europe.

A crucial stage is reached when the newly passed state law

setting the work week at fifty-four hours goes into effect. Under Ditmar's urging, the mill owners have decided to reduce their employees' pay proportionately with the reduction in working hours. Despite warnings of a strike, Ditmar believes he can handle any situation and accepts one of the largest orders in history for his textile mill at the precise time the reduced work week goes into effect.

On the Monday following Janet's and Lise's separate trips to Boston, the workers in the Hampton mills go on strike. Janet's concern at Lise's situation and her own recognition that she has been a victim of Ditmar's determination to achieve whatever he wants force her to break with her lover and to join the strike. Believing now that Ditmar never intends to marry her, she sees, after all, that her interests lie more with the workers than with the mill agent. Thus Churchill brings the personal and the socio-economic issues together.

The Hampton strike is quickly taken over by the syndicalist movement represented by the "Wobblies." Janet joins the head-quarters staff of their local unit through a newly acquired friendship with one of the syndicalist leaders, the intellectual but Bohemian Leonard Rolfe. Rolfe, who says he will educate her to syndicalism, suggests readings for her and discusses with her the class struggle and the rise of the proletariat. But it soon becomes apparent that he associates free love with the radical cause. Rolfe has found a new woman with every strike; this time, he assumes Janet is to be his associate in sexual freedom. But Janet, already victimized once, sees through Rolfe long before he can talk her into a second seduction. She is quickly disillusioned with both syndicalism and its bright young representative.

When Janet learns she is to bear a child by Ditmar, she is thrown into such consternation that she determines to kill him and herself. At the last moment, when she confronts him, she cannot go through with it and flees to the sanctuary of a third male protagonist who has flitted briefly through the story from the beginning. This is the mystical writer Brooks Insall, who has learned to live above the world's strife, who sympathizes with the workers but is immune to causes and movements. Insall is a man with enough private means to remain in the ivory tower of idealism.

Janet's shock when she learns her sister's willingness to become a prostitute, her realization of her own decision to murder Ditmar, and her pregnancy lead her to a nervous breakdown. Insall and his friend, Mrs. Maturin, take Janet to nearby Silliston, an academic town that has always appealed to Janet as the epitome of order and beauty. There, under their attention, she slowly recovers.

Churchill moves his story rapidly in the last few chapters. It soon develops that Insall has fallen in love with Janet, the third man in the book to do so; but she must reject him because of the child that is on the way—and also because she now discovers she really loved Ditmar all the time and that he really loved her. When she arrives at this belated conclusion, it is too late to do anything about it because Ditmar is dead, the victim of a demented assassin. Her only recourse is to accept the help offered by Mrs. Maturin, to reject Insall, and to flee from the prying eyes of society to the Maturin camp in the Canadian North Woods to have her child. In the last chapter, Janet learns that Insall knows her secret and that he still wishes to marry her. But she feels this impulse is prompted only by his generosity and she will not accept it. She confides to Mrs. Maturin that she knows she will not recover from the childbirth. Mrs. Maturin promises to take the newborn daughter and, with the help of Brooks Insall, to rear it as her own. Thus, in what turned out to be his last novel, Churchill ends on a sober note.

The reaction of the critics to Churchill's last and most radical novel was confused and contradictory. Some scarcely recognized the earlier genteel author of the historical romances. The *Outlook* found that "Mr. Churchill is not afraid to present life as it is, and that with unsparing frankness."[12] The *Independent* said he was trying to imitate Theodore Dreiser, a role he was ill-equipped to play. "Mr. Churchill is a sheep in wolf's clothing, and the costume suits him not at all."[13] The *Catholic World* regretted that Churchill, at a time of national peril, would offer a "defense of the propaganda of syndicalism and mob-rule." But the Socialist New York *Call* interpreted the message differently and was displeased for quite the opposite reason: "The preachment . . . against socialistic and syndicalistic ideas smacks of that mid-McKinleyan conservatism and prudery out of whose somber shadows America has stepped, for once and for all."[14] H. W.

Boynton, reviewing the novel for both the *Bookman* and the *Nation,* found the scenic descriptions of the New England town admirable, but he felt that Churchill had offered no real solution to the questions he posed. In Boynton's view, the author had abandoned the real problem and taken refuge in the personal human story of Janet Bumpus.[15] "We might have wished something more in the direction of a solution than its vague appeal to the standards of rural-academic culture."[16] Francis Hackett in the *New Republic,* however, saw the novel as an attempt to explain the Lawrence strike to the children of gentility. He found nothing shocking in the book; instead, he found it a further example of Churchill's success, "the tenacity of his Americanistic vitality."[17] In general, English reviewers were kinder than the American.

Two things that some of the critics observed still stand out in *The Dwelling-Place of Light.* One is that Churchill moved in this novel as far into the path of literary naturalism as his own nature would let him. A book with two seductions, a planned abortion, a murder, and another contemplated murder-suicide, it is far removed from the juvenile fiction of the historical romances. True, these sordid situations are treated for the most part with the circumspect approach of the earlier genteel tradition; nevertheless, they are there. And Churchill is clear enough in using seduction as the focal point of the novel. In the emphasis on the tawdry background of the Bumpus home and in his concern with the details in the first two-thirds of the book, Churchill approaches Dreiser. Indeed, Janet Bumpus reminds one of Jennie Gerhardt or Carrie Meeber, although at the end of the book she is more sophisticated and certainly more intellectual than either of the Dreiser heroines.

The second and more interesting thing about *The Dwelling-Place of Light* is the dichotomy of Churchill's attitude toward militant radicalism. Certainly, he has moved further to the left in this book than in any other. Always his sympathies are with the workers as opposed to the owners. And the reader feels that Churchill is almost convinced of a Marxist-socialist approach as he has Rolfe discuss syndicalism. But like Janet Bumpus, Churchill changes his mind at the last moment; his answer is not syndicalism, not radicalism, but a cloudy idealism that again shows his reluctance to relinquish what he considered the American tradition. Churchill is now convinced of the essential nature of the class struggle; he no longer blames a nation's woes solely on wicked or evil men. He sees clearly that more is at stake than a change of heart or a change of owners. The system that produces such owners is at fault and needs some adjustment. Yet, he cannot accept the answer of the Industrial Workers of the World.

Churchill is too much the product, if not the epitome, of his own genteel-romantic-Progressive age to turn to the radical for a solution. In fact, he knows no solution other than to fall back on the romantic answers. In *A Far Country* it is science that seems to point the way; in *The Dwelling-Place of Light* it is the ivory-towered idealism represented in Brooks Insall. Charles Walcutt has maintained that Churchill "could not carry his study through to the conclusions which were so plainly indicated by his presentation of the problem."[18] This inability was due to Churchill's never going beyond the Progressive Party answer in his novels; for, it is always important to remember, Churchill was not a leader but a reflection of majority Progressive thought. In groping for hesitant solutions that frequently proved inadequate, he was in step with most of the political leaders of his time. After all, Theodore Roosevelt was no radical; some would even question that he was a genuine liberal during his years as President. It was Woodrow Wilson's attorney-general who pushed the Big Red Scare, and it was during Wilson's administration that Eugene Debs was jailed. Most of the Progressive novelists were like Roosevelt and Wilson—in reality, they were very moderate men who proposed no far-reaching or radical solutions to the conditions they exposed. Not until the New Deal of the 1930's was the country really ready to come to grips with the issues posed by the industrial and business expansion of the twentieth century.

But if Churchill did not have the answers, he must be credited, at least, with recognizing the problems. Unlike Booth Tarkington, he did not bury his head in the sand or smile economic difficulties away with middle-class complacency. He was sincere; he was concerned. He knew not what direction to take, shunning the trodden road but hoping always to find the way on a path where the sunshine of American traditions might glow. As it was, his economic novels foreshadow the proletarian fiction of the 1930's, the world of Dos Passos and of Steinbeck.

Churchill does an admirable job in *The Dwelling-Place of Light* of painting the picture of the Lawrence strike and of showing the confusion and degradation into which the European immigrants were forced after their arrival in the textile community. The antagonism of the older, Puritan-descended resident to the new immigrant hordes is clearly indicated—even when the "pure" American is almost as economically depressed as his European cohort. The first two-thirds of the book is, in fact, an admirable piece of mildly naturalistic writing from the standpoint of depicting environment and its deadening effect on its subjects. Dreiser, generally considered one of the leading American naturalists, did no better.

The last third of the novel, however, is marred by contrivance. As indicated before, Churchill apparently did not know how to solve the economic problem he had posed, so he rushed pell-mell into an ending that is neither plausible nor convincing. One suspects it would be difficult to persuade a starving striker that the answer to his woes lies in reading the newer economists and in withdrawing to a neutralist's position of idealistic aloofness. No doubt, there was too much materialism in the striker's approach to his problem and in the owner's concern with profits. Yet, one must have sufficient means of support to become a disinterested observer of the passing parade of life. Families must still be fed, children clothed and educated. Brooks Insall could afford to remain aloof from causes; the average mill hand in Hampton could not. As for Janet Bumpus, her solution was to die—scarcely an appealing escape for the mass of humanity.

Aside from the early portrayal of Janet Bumpus, there is nothing noteworthy in the character delineation in the book. The dialogue is less flamboyant than in *The Inside of the Cup,* but it still too often has the characteristics of formal address. The book is long, even though it does not meander so much as *A Far Country.* The first two-thirds is concerned largely with the Janet Bumpus-Claude Ditmar romance, with overtones of the larger economic issues hovering in the background. It takes too long to reach the climax. When it comes, Churchill crowds too much into the last few chapters. The plot, more realistic and more appealing in its outline than many another that Churchill contrived, becomes in its execution threadbare and unconvincing. Again, it is the larger panorama—the setting, the description, the portrayal of large groups of people representative of a segment of society—that vindicates the novel. The individual characters are quickly forgotten; the over-all picture remains.

In both *A Far Country* and *The Dwelling-Place of Light* it is clear that Churchill had read much and studied deeply in the fields of economics and sociology. Not only in the references to the Manchester school of economics, the syndicalist movement, Bergson, or William James is this evident, but also in the arguments Churchill advances through his characters. That he found ready answers in what he had studied, or that he achieved any lasting satisfaction with the newer economics, is questionable. Better able to absorb and understand history than contemporary events, he was essentially a romantic adrift, after 1910, in the alien realm of social problems. The result was confused answers reflected in dwindling book sales. Except for *The Inside of the Cup,* his success with the public steadily declined after *Mr. Crewe's Career.* Though he interested himself in the usual problems of the Progressive, it was evident by 1917 that he was beginning to lose his touch with the American reader. Yet, so impelled was he by a concern with the issues he saw about him, so sincere was he in his writing endeavors, that he was determined to go on probing for the solution at the same time that he hinted in his novels that he had found it.

Meanwhile, America was thrust into World War I; domestic reform was pushed aside in the fight to save democracy; and Progressivism went into a decline from which it did not emerge for fifteen years. Churchill found his readers concerned no longer with Progressive matters, but with the world-wide struggle against Germany. Churchill, too, in the spirit of times, decided to join the war effort. He determined to offer his services to the Navy Department in Washington for whatever use they might be. The immediate result was a trip abroad followed by a volume of travel essays; but the long-term and more significant result was an alteration of tone and interest of such magnitude as to change the writer's future direction and to end abruptly his professional career.

CHAPTER 7

The Late Years

I

LIKE MANY of the Progressives, Winston Churchill was slow to awaken to the crisis of World War I. His published writings before 1917 reflect no concern with political events in Europe. Several years earlier, he, like his friend Theodore Roosevelt, had visited Kaiser Wilhelm II in Germany and had found him an effective, courageous leader that an American could admire. Despite his fiction which frequently displayed a sympathy for the economic underdog, Churchill was sometimes responsive to the social forms of royalty and aristocracy, and the Kaiser's court in Berlin was one of several that had impressed him on his European tours. Unlike Roosevelt, Churchill had not urged immediate involvement of the United States in the war when it came. He also parted company with the former President because of his own general regard for Woodrow Wilson. Churchill's respect for the Democratic President grew steadily from the first two summers when the Wilsons rented "Harlakenden House" until 1918 when the author publicly eulogized Wilson and his plan for a League of Nations.

When President Wilson led the nation into the war in April, 1917, Churchill was an enthusiastic supporter who was quick to lend his service to the war effort. In 1917, Churchill was forty-six years old. It was obvious that a man of his talents and age could best serve the nation with his pen. The Secretary of the Navy, Josephus Daniels, suggested that Churchill's Naval Academy training qualified him as an observer and public interpreter of the navy. Consequently, much of Churchill's effort during the war was devoted to propagandizing the role of the fleet in Allied victory.

As early as June, 1917, the navy asked Churchill to write an article in support of a Marine Corps drive to recruit four thousand men during the week of June 11. The article, "A Call for the Marine Corps," appeared in the New York *Times* on June 14. A highly patriotic piece, it related some high points in the history of the Marines, and suggested that the corpsmen were not enough appreciated by their fellow countrymen. The article was accompanied by an announcement that Churchill was becoming "a sort of scribe for the Navy" in the war effort.[1]

A more significant article was "Naval Organization, American and British" which appeared in the *Atlantic* for August, 1917. Again urging Americans to take a more active interest in their navy, he outlined the organizational pattern of the Navy Department and contrasted it with the British system. He complained of the "nefarious system of checks and balances that plagued the U. S. government"[2] and was pessimistic about American ability to overcome the submarine menace. Interestingly, too, he voiced criticisms of Winston S. Churchill, who had been First Lord of the Admiralty in Great Britain between 1911 and 1915 and had been the subject of considerable controversy, particularly during 1915, because of the nature of his naval policy and the failure of the Dardanelles campaign. The American had talked with the British Naval Commission when it came to this country shortly after the United States entered the war; he was thoroughly familiar with the arguments surrounding the English Churchill.

By the end of the summer of 1917, Churchill was off to Europe to view the war zones and to report as a semi-official representative of the Navy Department. He went first to France, then to Britain and Ireland, and finally returned to France. He was back in America by early 1918, and his written observations started to appear serially in *Scribner's* magazine in February of that year.[3] In July, 1918, Macmillan decided to publish the articles with an added essay on "The American Contribution and the Democratic Idea." The book bore the title *A Traveller in War-Time.*

This series of essays, Churchill's major contribution to the literature of the war effort, won immediate praise from the critics. The last essay in particular, in which the author set forth some discriminating comment on the American national character, won the plaudits of readers. In the first chapters, he simply relates his impressions of France and England in war-time. As an historian of the romantic school, Churchill invests the battlefields of Vimy Ridge, Arras, and the Somme with the glow of a travelogue rather than with the realism of war. The book is full of praise for the Allies—particularly the British. He had dined with Lloyd George, Sir James Barrie, and H. G. Wells, and he had found all three highly stimulating companions. He had also met with Admiral Sims and other American Naval officials. To the Americans at home, he wrote that they need not fear for the welfare of their boys and that he had changed his mind about the ability of the United States to defeat the submarine.

But what impressed Churchill most and what he waxed most enthusiastic about was the new revolutionary social sentiment that he saw exemplified in the British Labour movement. He had seen Sidney Webb and discussed Fabian Socialism with him. It is a consciousness of social ferment that he puts into his essay on "The American Contribution and the Democratic Idea." Pointing out that industrial democracy is the real issue of the time, Churchill believes the new Labour forces in Britain are outlining the solution that the Progressives had earlier been seeking, but could not find, in America. He sees the Labour Party pointing the way toward a complete renovation of society itself, toward an organization based on the principles and ideas of Christianity. He believes the war may be the catalytic agent to force the necessary socializing changes that are coming in America. He is confident there will be a new religious emphasis and that the United States' greatest contribution to the total postwar world may be to enforce a recognition of universal education as the cornerstone of a socialized democracy. (He is, at this point, strong in his praise of John Dewey.)

The book reflects Churchill's growing endorsement of Woodrow Wilson. He commends the President for daring to cast aside outworn elements of the social structure and speaks highly of Wilson's war ideals, acknowledging him as "the democratic leader of the world."[4] But to achieve the kind of optimistic future that *A Traveller in War-Time* envisions, Churchill casts aside both of the old political parties and calls for the formation of a Liberal Party based on the findings of modern social science.[5] With unchecked optimism, he practically foresees the

millennium—the end result of all his social and economic probing in the problem novels. Of course, it was not to be. The
election of 1920 and the events that followed close after the end
of the war must have dismayed and sobered him.

II

During . much of 1918 Churchill suffered from ill health
and had to lay aside his pen. By the time he had recovered, the
war was over and his assignment of naval correspondent ex-
officio was ended. He had not, however, lost his interest in
social and economic problems, as his first publication after the
war revealed. In December, 1918, he contributed an introduction
to a pamphlet called "St. Louis After the War," a promotional
tract prepared by the St. Louis City Planning Commission. The
introduction was published later in *American City* (January,
1919) as "The Supreme Question Facing Our City and Country
Today." While the main purpose of the article was to urge
support of St. Louis postwar plans for development, the author
spoke in much broader terms of the new function of science,
particularly of psychology, in bringing about an awareness and
solution of the industrial problems of postwar cities. He hoped
that the ideal gained in the war could be applied to the reconstruction of cities like St. Louis. Once again, he spoke of the
true issue of the war as the necessity of "socializing and
democratizing the modern industrial community."[6]

Churchill's continuing interest in industrial democracy was
even more pronounced in a play he actually wrote before the
war ended, although it was not published until September, 1919.
Churchill had flirted with the theater for years. All of the
historical novels had been dramatized, and in 1906 he had
written and produced a three-act light comedy called "The
Title-Mart" that satirized the marriage matches between the
idle rich of England and America. Through the years, he had
also toyed with stage versions of the political novels. Like Henry
James, he never did his best work in drama but he could never
quite escape its lure. It was no new thing, therefore, for him
to turn playwright. But this time his purpose was to be clearly
didactic; he meant to preach the new social democracy in
his play.

Dr. Jonathan concerns Asher Pindar, inheritor and owner of the Pindar Manufacturing Plant in Foxon Falls, New England; George Pindar, his son; and Dr. Jonathan Pindar, his cousin. Asher and his wife Augusta are of the old-fashioned school of industrial relations, believing in the paternalistic system of *noblesse oblige*. Asher feels that he is entitled to all the profit he can get, although he carefully looks after the welfare of his workers. Opposed to labor unions, he vows he will never recognize the attempt of his workers to organize. Augusta, one of the feminine adornments of the wealthy man's home, takes no part in Asher's business dealings but confines herself to church work and mild philanthropy. George Pindar, the son, has more liberal views than his parents. He is on much friendlier terms with the workers in his father's shops than is Asher, and he is not above fraternizing with the shop foreman's daughter, an Irish miss named Minnie Farrell. Old Timothy Farrell, Minnie's father, is loyal to his thirty-year master, Asher Pindar, and he opposes the movement in the plant to organize the workers into an American Federation of Labor union.

Things have reached a crisis in Act I when George is about to leave his parents for the battlefields of France. His leave-taking is disturbed by the threat of a strike in the plant unless Asher recognizes the union. At this point, Jonathan Pindar, cousin of Asher, appears. He is an idealistic doctor dedicated to medical research and the well-being of his fellowmen. Jonathan sees that one issue of the war, economic freedom for all, has already reached Foxon Falls; and he plants the seeds of social science in the mind of young George as he is about to set off for war. The lad leaves, torn between filial affection and recognition that his father is wrong in opposing the unions.

Meanwhile, Minnie Farrell has turned away from the religious indoctrination of Augusta and has sought a gayer life in the city of Newcastle where she has found escape from the boredom of factory routine. She has temporarily returned to Foxon Falls for a "sentimental visit" in time to say farewell to George, object of her earlier flirtations. Dr. Jonathan, who sees Minnie's real worth, takes her on as an assistant and practical nurse in the new laboratory-clinic he has come to establish in the community.

All during Act II, George writes home to his father urging him to recognize the union and to acknowledge the twentieth century. George sees the war as a struggle for the oppressed laborers of all nations and holds the hope that the postwar world may be "reorganized on some intelligent basis."[7] He warns his father that economic inequalities must be reduced and that new opportunities for "living" must be offered the toilers. But the father sticks to his old-fashioned principles of property rights and benevolent business autocracy. He considers the threat of his workers to strike in wartime as nothing short of treason.

In the last act, George comes home from the war a shell-shock victim. The strike, which has been averted for nine months and two acts, has now taken place. When the son sees that his father has not heeded the messages he has been sending from the battle fronts, he is seized by another nervous relapse. Dr. Jonathan, who takes over the case, warns old Asher that he must give in to his son's views and recognize the union if he wishes to see him survive and recuperate. Asher relents at the last moment to save his son's health—but not because of any fundamental change in his own views. The strike is called off; one is certain that George will now be restored to normal; and the promise of a new industrial experiment along socialistic lines is assured when Asher abdicates and turns the business over to his liberal son. To complete the ending, George persuades Minnie to marry him—Minnie, the poor daughter of the plant foreman who feels she is too far beneath her lover to become his wife. But George assures her that she is his cultural equal. Minnie is finally convinced; and, together, they will spend their time in the new industrial experiment of Foxon Falls rather than on the Wall Street-Palm Beach circuit that might have been George's inheritance.

As dramatic art, *Dr. Jonathan* is hardly worth considering. (Only the socialistic New York *Call* had kind words for the play in its time.) As an index to Churchill's thinking, however, the play is important. Seldom read today, it indicates that Churchill had gone further down the economic road he had started under the Progressives than many contemporary historians thought. When Churchill hopefully suggested that an economic system free of capitalist exploiters could be forged out of the war, he further extended the industrial democracy he had hinted at in *A Far Country* and in *The Dwelling-Place of Light;* and he revealed the kind of thinking that was increasingly out of step with the popular concepts of the country.

The author was, indeed, finding himself without an audience. Roosevelt had died in January, 1919. With him, though not because of him, died many of the Progressive issues of the prewar years. With most of its earlier objectives achieved, the heart of Progressivism rapidly waned in the face of postwar developments. Churchill himself was careful to point out that he was not really advocating a radical solution. With sound argument, he appealed for a liberal answer to the industrial problems of the day before a radical movement were thrust upon the nation to create more chaos than it succeeded in eliminating. In the Preface to *Dr. Jonathan*, Churchill foresaw that the war had unleashed forces that would have to be dealt with. Across the Atlantic, these forces burst into the Red Revolution. But in America, conformity and "normalcy" were to regain the ascendancy the next fall in the election of 1920. Churchill was far too optimistic in his appraisal of what the war might do. The United States had to await the Great Depression and the New Deal of another Roosevelt before Churchill's prophecy for an industrial democracy could be approached. Meanwhile, he had gone beyond his middle-class reading public. *Dr. Jonathan* dealt with the highly explosive subject of labor relations in a way that was becoming increasingly suspect by 1919. Not that it mattered to Churchill, but, for the first time in his life, he was no longer in tune with his times.

III

Dr. Jonathan, the last Churchill book to come from the Macmillan press, represented the beginning of a twenty-two-year self-imposed literary silence for Churchill.[8] In fact, the story of Churchill the practicing author actually ends about 1920; for after this date, he seems to have had little interest in being a writer, successful or otherwise. It remains only to record the last years and the peculiar religious tangent he pursued that culminated in one final book.

With the publication of *The Inside of the Cup*, Churchill had taken to the pulpit. Reading and refining his thought, he kept his Christianity, but it steadily left the precincts of the organized faiths and emerged into something that was distinctly his own, though he thought of it as growing out of modern science. During his residence in California, Churchill had developed an interest in psychology as it applied to spiritual matters. By April, 1917, the crystallization of his religious speculation had led him to write the Episcopal Bishop of New Hampshire that he could no longer accept the statements of a supernatural character in Christianity and he implied that the tenets of Episcopal theology were no longer compatible with his thinking. Eventually he was to reach what Kenneth Cameron has called "a faith in self-abnegating Christian love and a Universalist or evolutionary theory concerning the after-life."[9]

On March 26, 1922, a curious piece by Churchill appeared in the New York *Times Book Review and Magazine.* Entitled "Two Minds for One," it must have amazed those of Churchill's former readers who saw it. In the article, he speaks of the "two distinct minds" of man—the primitive and the creative.[10] The primitive, which has its location somewhere along the backbone, is concerned with the basic instincts, including acquisition and possession. The creative, seated in the brain, is instinctively directed toward emotional identity with other minds—toward love. This love toward others, living or dead, in its highest phase is exemplified in man's everyday relations. No longer is the individual concerned with advocating new social doctrines with a view to changing the organization of society; rather, he is transformed by love into a selfless individual contributor to the social weal.

Churchill maintains that there is an eternal conflict between the primitive and creative minds. This conflict he calls "sentimentalism." A scientific approach to religion would insure that the creative would supplant the primitive emotions. Christ had the scientific mind, not the mystic, Churchill argues. His truths were rational truths, the result of the creative mind expressing the whole personality. Christ preached a psychology that was essentially creative, not primitive. But His doctrines, in the hands of the church, have "wallowed in sentimentalism" throughout the centuries. In his denunciation of the church, Churchill was particularly scathing. The church is interested only in material power, not spiritual; hence it fails to be influential in a scientific age.

As near as can be determined, the *Times* article met with silence. Churchill's religious speculations and, more specifically, his attack on the church hit the very segment of the reading public that had heretofore been his main strength, and at a time when religious liberalism was suffering a decline similar to other Progressive sentiments. It was clear that Churchill would enjoy no mass audiences in the unpropitious decade of the 1920's.

Two Churchill magazine articles of this period had the same fate as the *Times* article. In April, 1922, he published "The Knowledge of Good and Evil" in the *North American Review* and "An Uncharted Way" in the *Yale Review;* both were more exalted attempts to present his notion of the dual mind of man. In the first article he is more specific about the primitive mind, as distinct from an "unconscious" or "subconscious." The primitive mind moves in syncopated rhythm with the beating of the heart and normally controls metabolism and digestion. The creative mind, on the other hand, moves in unsyncopated rhythm with breathing and the brain and is concerned with "the digestion of experience."[11] Churchill may have further alienated his middle-class audience when he wrote of sex as "the main-spring of creative forces."[12] He went on to attack traditional morality and traditional beliefs of good and evil as being unscientifically founded.

Churchill was again reading his psychology. His writings suggest an acquaintance with Freud. He mentions Francis Galton, and evidently he had recently gone over William James's *Varieties of Religious Experience,* for in the *Yale Review* article he praises James's views. The *Yale Review* essay, however, is even more curious and more puzzling than the *North American Review* piece. It argues for immortality and for the continuing influence that a great love, though deceased, can have on the living. There is more than a hint of spiritualism in a number of passages, but the over-all tone indicates that Churchill was primarily concerned with combining some ideas in contemporary psychology with his own highly individualized religious concepts.

These articles suggest that the creator of Richard Carvel and Stephen Brice had come a long way indeed, though his audience had failed to follow him. But if the public could not assimilate Churchill's new thought, he at least was not at all distracted or distressed. For religion became the dominant interest of his life for twenty-five years. Abandoning the field of fiction altogether, he became concerned until his death with working out a new interpretation of the gospels. For this purpose, he undertook the study of Greek and Hebrew and endeavored to translate the Old and New Testaments from their original sources. He was enthusiastic in his pursuit, but was largely unconcerned about expounding his doctrines for the large audiences he had earlier reached. The old Churchill was gone; the new craved few readers or listeners. Gradually, his retirement brought him the obscurity he now seemed to desire.

Life at "Harlakenden House" underwent a change. Gone were the days of gala entertainment. The endless round of guests that in the past had included notables from the world of business and finance, the arts and literature, the diplomatic corps, and even two Presidents of the United States, was superseded by the quiet of a modest, retiring man residing in the midst of a simpler household. In 1923, the house burned to the ground. The cause of the fire was not determined, but Churchill must not have been too sorry to see it go. It represented the old prewar world—a world that was gone from his mind as he turned to other pursuits.

The Churchills moved into another dwelling that stood to the north of "Harlakenden House" on their own property. Here they were to remain until the end. Churchill took up painting in some earnestness, though solely as an avocation. He had dabbled at the art for years, but in the 1920's and 1930's it became a real pursuit with him and he achieved some minor success with it. In these years he also spent much time in carpentry and in general shop work, since he found such things a relaxation from the mental activity his translations of the gospels brought him.

As for writing, there was little of it—none of a professional nature—between 1922 and 1940. In 1931, Churchill told Phoebe Storms, an inquiring student, that writing novels had only been a hobby with him, and that he was not particularly proud of the results he had achieved. "With a twinkle in his eyes he adds that *he* 'takes novels' only when he wants to be drugged," Miss Storms reported.[13] He told another inquirer: "I ceased writing novels at the age of forty-six because I enjoyed living quietly on my country place, dabbling in painting and reading the works of others, writing occasionally for my own satisfaction, and the pleasure of a few intimates, to whom I gave carbon copies of my typed manuscripts. To the world I said that it was a question of fun and that I derived more fun living as I did, apart, painting and carpentering." Significantly, he added, "It is very difficult now for me to think of myself as a writer of novels, as all that seems to belong to another life. And I never was really literary. I wrote the novel for pleasure or adventure."[14] During these years he repudiated most of his best-selling problem novels and became almost as harsh in his evaluation of them as his severest critics had been.

Churchill was much less in the news after 1920. In 1924, Mrs. Churchill mildly astonished the press by supporting the Democratic nominee, John W. Davis, for the Presidency. Churchill himself, a former active Republican and Progressive, seemed no longer interested in politics. In 1925, he created a minor flurry with the publishers by maintaining that the price of books was excessive and adding that he was "fed up with the modern purveyors of books." "I won't turn loose the stories I have written for myself, to be sold at high prices to people who won't appreciate them."[15] This brought forth the inevitable replies from publishers plus a few newspaper editorials, some in support of Churchill's contention and others aligned with the publishers. Walter J. Black did offer at the time to publish any new Churchill novel at a selling price of one dollar, but the author did not respond.[16]

In fact, in 1930, Churchill told an audience at Nantucket that he did not ever expect to write again. "I'm more content in private life with easel and canvas, adze and hammer. Do you know I've almost forgotten that I ever did write? I never thought much of books anyway." He added a note about his own fading position in literature: "Life goes according to fashions and fads. . . . The world becomes too much a slave of the present mode, forgetting that there ever was any other. And that is the reason that I am out of step with the world."[17] By and large, he had disappeared from the public view as the years slipped rapidly away. It was something of a surprise to reviewers, therefore, when he burst into print again in 1940 after a twenty-year silence.

IV

All during the late 1930's, much of Churchill's energy was centered on relating psychic research to Christian teaching. He sought to apply scientific principles to the gospels in order to arrive at the true teaching of Christ, which he believed had been thoroughly distorted by the organized church. With no book that he ever wrote did Churchill struggle more than with the last. *The Uncharted Way,* finally published in 1940 after months of effort and reworking, broke Churchill's long literary silence, but it created scarcely a critical or popular ripple.

Written in essay form, the chief message is an appeal for a non-contentious philosophy that is akin to the passive resistance of Gandhi or to the Christian doctrine of Tolstoy. But before arriving at this thesis, Churchill laboriously examines the history of Christian doctrine and tries to show that Christ and, later, the apostle Paul were actually suggesting a path based on an acute understanding of human psychology and the innate creative instincts of man. Churchill maintains that every individual is endowed with a moral self and a technical or rebellious self; for spiritual integrity, a reconciliation of both selves is necessary. However, under the prevailing Christian dispensations the moral self has been stressed. The moral self means that society operates according to a law of works. As long as the individual makes proper obeisance to God and recognizes God as the true owner of all property, God, in turn, confers upon the individual the right of stewardship for his property. By propitiating the Deity, in other words, one gains the right to acquire and hold goods in meeting material needs.

This system works very well until the spirit of rebellion, the technical self, asserts itself. There is then a complete re-examination of the nature of society, frequently in the direction of more liberal, democratic government, accompanied by religious liberalism, if not downright skepticism. Churchill suggests such upheavels occurred during the reigns of Ikhnaton in Egypt, during the Golden Age of Greece, at the time of the Renaissance, and in the Protestant Reformation. At such times, the reliance is on science and on man's capacities as "a technical creature."[18]

Churchill believes that the ancient prophets had suggested a way to the reconciliation of these two basic human impulses in pointing out a type of creative life energy that would be based on inspirational love (*agape*).[19] Jesus re-emphasized the message; Paul also enunciated it. But in every instance they failed to communicate their notions to their immediate followers, just as they failed with the masses. The essential, dynamic message of the gospels, therefore, has been ignored.

In elaborating on his notions of just what this life energy is, Churchill falters. He implies that it is somehow associated with artistic instinct, with creative zeal. He also suggests a kind of universalist evolutionary theory that will usher in an eventual millennium on the "third day"—that era when man shall finally reconcile his conflicting selves in a Law of Faith manifested by non-contentious love. But there is much circumlocution in his discussion, and most of the message is hidden in the turgid prose of his scholarly style.

Throughout the book, Churchill displays his new knowledge of Greek and the classics. He is careful to point out the true derivations of words and the faulty meanings which translators of the gospels have been guilty of perpetuating. He also gives some peculiarly new twists to the parables of the gospels, displaying, perhaps, the results of his religious investigations which had led him to paths quite alien to the usual theological interpretations. Over the whole book, he throws an aura of science and psychological implication partly occasioned, at least, by his reading of William James's *Varieties of Religious Experience*.

In a letter to Phoebe Storms, Churchill wrote that he thought of *The Uncharted Way* as a new interpretation of the gospel doctrine "for which I take no personal credit, as I think such things must be regarded as gifts." He recognized that the book was difficult and that few people would make the attempt to grasp its meaning. This, however, did not disturb him. "It took me twenty years to write, during which time I made experiments with the non-contentious behavior in order to discover for myself what science and psychology might underlie it. . . . I am interested only in those who desire to read the book with this end, as a science of psychology which they will adopt in order to reach a third stage of human experience."[20]

True to the author's expectations, *The Uncharted Way* had only a small sale and never went beyond the first printing.[21]

Only a few publications bothered to review it, and it seems probable that Churchill's earlier reputation was all that saved it from utter oblivion. John Haynes Holmes in the New York *Herald-Tribune* stated that Churchill had lost his literary touch in the two decades of his silence. He found the book confused and doubted its soundness. He particularly attacked the "dubious derivations of familiar words from classic tongues" and the "surprising, if not inaccurate, interpretations of scripture." Acknowledging that Churchill had some ideas, Holmes said the author did not know what to do with them. "For all the book's earnestness and deep sincerity, it gets us nowhere. The 'way', so far as Mr. Churchill is concerned, is still 'uncharted.' "[22]

The *Christian Century* warned its readers to remember that this was not the work of the British Prime Minister, a precaution that was, in itself, an indication of the American Churchill's changed position in the world. Down to 1920, any such explanation would have been unnecessary. The reviewer then summarized Churchill's argument and remarked that "one gathers the present work did not come from his hand in precisely the form in which it is presented."[23]

Time magazine summarized Churchill's theories and commented that the book "is the work of a stonily independent amateur thinker." It warned against too hasty a dismissal of Churchill's effort, however, and suggested that "he who finds in it mere idiocy may perhaps be mistaken."[24]

Churchill was not abashed by the reaction to *The Uncharted Way.* He had always written more for fun and for teaching than for profit, albeit he considered his thinking now of far more significance than his earlier didactic attempts. No more was he trying to effect reform. *The Uncharted Way* reveals that the novel of propaganda was far from his thoughts. No longer did he believe that the Kingdom of Heaven could be put into an organization. He did not foresee a perfected social order in this world; if there was to be a perfection of individuals it would have to take place in another dispensation. Perhaps the political experience of the 1920's or the new directions that literature took after World War I had brought a change in his outlook. Events in his own personal life also contributed to this change. Certainly, the man who wrote *The Uncharted Way* was quite a different person from the one who published a best-selling problem novel every two years between 1908 and 1918; and he bore scarcely any resemblance to the historian of *Richard Carvel* or *The Crisis*. The same enthusiasm was there, but the focus was altogether different.

V

Churchill lived in modesty and relative obscurity in his late years. During the 1920's and 1930's, he had been recognized in the anthologies and in the literary histories. The *International Book Review* in 1924 had named him fourth in a list of the greatest writers appearing after 1900.[25] Four of his books had been listed in Asa Dickinson's *One Thousand Best Books* in 1931.[26] But after World War II, he was scarcely mentioned.

Churchill died from a heart attack at Winter Park, Florida, on March 12, 1947, long after he had passed from the contemporary literary scene. It was a surprise to a younger generation of Americans who read the obituaries to discover that there had been another Winston Churchill, an American, who had been, according to report, almost as famous in his day as the former British Prime Minister was currently. But there must have been a momentary stir in the hearts of many people of an older generation who had read his books by the millions of copies. The New York *Times* editorialized, "In 1900, even after the British Churchill had been taken prisoner by the Boers and dramatically escaped, there was no question in this country as to which Churchill was *the* Winston Churchill. . . . He was American to the heart, deeply feeling and warmly expressing a great tradition. His political career, in the Bull Moose days, won him no high office, but showed him to be a courageous liberal. All who now read historical fiction and all who write it owe much to him."[27] The New York *Herald-Tribune* recalled that *Richard Carvel* and *The Crisis* had been the most popular romances of their time and had brought their author well-deserved fame at an early age. "Millions of readers have gained fun and instruction from his books. If history needs to be made a gilded pill for a people's ready swallowing, in three brilliant American novels Winston Churchill's gilding was enduring gold, applied with a sure and careful touch."[28]

The man who had disappointed so many readers when, at the age of forty-six, he put aside his pen and went into literary retirement had now passed from the scene. Taken to his home in New Hampshire, he was buried beside his wife who had died two years before in 1945. In a solitary private lot near the site of "Harlakenden House," his grave is today removed from public attention and visitation. No doubt he would prefer it that way. Yet one cannot help noting the ironic destiny of a man who at the height of his career, before his withdrawal from the world of popular authorship, was one of the most lionized writers in America. Few celebrated men have lived to see their names so totally eclipsed as did the American Churchill—and few men probably have cared less.

CHAPTER 8

Epilogue

I

THE CAREER of Winston Churchill suggests two questions: Why did an eminently successful author suddenly retire from the world of literature? And what is the place in the story of American civilization today of an author whose reputation has declined as markedly as Churchill's?

Churchill's abandonment of his successful career as a novelist was more a matter of the man than of the times. "I stopped reading as well as writing novels in 1917 when my interest turned to other things," he said in 1947.[1] Even before World War I he had started to turn steadily from the exterior world of social and economic reform to the interior realms of religion and psychology. Churchill had always written because he enjoyed narration and because he burned with an idea to profess. His thinking in the 1920's and 1930's took much longer to develop and could not be projected in fiction. Largely oblivious to politics and social conditions, he turned to the inner life of man.[2] In *The Uncharted Way* writing interested him only as a vehicle for the slow working out of his own religious answer. History and politics had been his early concerns; religion was his last.

Nevertheless, although his retirement from writing was primarily a matter involving his own interests and personality, two factors of the political and literary times cannot be ignored. The political climate of the post-World War I era changed markedly from what it had been before the war. The old Progressivism was broken up by the foreign entanglements of the 1918 period.[3] The return to "normalcy" in 1920 put the finishing touches to the clamor for conformity that had grown with a precipitate pace at the same time that liberals of the Churchill school were seeing the World War I venture as a different kind of struggle—as one more nearly akin to Wilson's effort to save democracy. Wilson's failure and disillusionment were very much their own. Churchill must have shared in the postwar dejection; and, like many of the Progressives, he soon deserted the field. John Chamberlain writes of the "farewell to reform" that occurred with America's entry into World War I,[4] and the *Survey Graphic* could inquire in 1926, "Where are the prewar radicals?"[5] Like Churchill, many of them were silent; they were shattered and subdued by the knowledge that liberalism had failed to carry the field at the crucial moment.

The changing nature of literary techniques in the period of "normalcy" may also have been an indirect factor in his decision to withdraw. The novel of reform, of social conscience, departed from the scene. The personal document of disillusionment and abandonment replaced it. Fitzgerald's *This Side of Paradise* ushered in the trend in 1920; Dos Passos' *Three Soldiers* (1921), Maxwell Anderson's and Laurence Stalling's *What Price Glory?* (1924), and Hemingway's *The Sun Also Rises* (1926) continued the pace. Fitzgerald, Dos Passos, both Andersons (Maxwell and Sherwood), and Hemingway were representative of a new school that was alien to Winston Churchill. He had tried to come to terms with prewar realism and, later, to a minor extent, with naturalism.[6] But always, he was basically a romantic. Admitting in 1914 that the realistic reaction had been of benefit to literature, he nonetheless felt that each author must continue in his own manner of expression.[7] In the prewar years, he had marched in solid company with historical fiction and the didactic problem novel. After World War I, these forces were scattered. Hence, Churchill put his pen down.

II

To trace critical comment on Churchill is to chart the steady decline of his reputation from the high point of 1910. Hamilton Mabie, Frederic T. Cooper, John C. Underwood, Horace Bridges, Charles C. Baldwin, Morris E. Speare, E. F. Harkins, and William Lyon Phelps are representative of earlier American literary historians who took Churchill seriously, although not always without adverse reaction. To read these critics is to ascertain the favorable contemporary evaluation of an author who Underwood said would always be paired with Thackeray. Thinking of Churchill's mastery of the larger canvas, Underwood wrote that his books were "big and vital enough to be judged first and last not as mere works of fiction and more or less successful products of literary art and artisanship, but as human documents and national studies in men and events of a very permanent and distinctive value."[8]

Taken as a whole, the critical receptions to his novels as they appeared added up to a similar judgment. Carl Van Doren in his *Contemporary American Novelists* (1922) devoted ten pages to Churchill, much of it critical; but he concluded with respect for the writer's earnestness and sincerity and, particularly, for his success in depicting American history. "He cannot be denied the honor of having added something agreeable if imponderable to the national memory and so of having served his country in one real way if not in another."[9] By 1940, however, when this earlier book was superseded by a revised edition of Van Doren's *The American Novel*, Churchill fared less well. A page-and-a-half summation was enough to dismiss him as "morally strenuous but intellectually belated."[10]

The Van Doren reaction is typical. During the 1920's, Churchill was still read and discussed, although he had dropped out of the public eye. The publication by Macmillan of the New Uniform Edition of the Churchill novels in 1927 indicated that interest in his work had not yet died. This edition also served to give his sagging reputation a small boost. Through the 1930's, however, as the Great Depression altered social and economic thinking the older generation began to forget the novels of its youth; a younger generation, at the same time, was concerned with the proletarian literature of a Steinbeck or of a Farrell. The public was hardly aware that this literature owed some debt to Churchill's precedent in *A Far Country* and *The Dwelling-Place of Light*. Fred Lewis Pattee in 1930 continued to view Churchill seriously by discussing him in six pages of his chapter called "Waverly Romance" in *The New American Literature*. By then, however, the three historical romances were deemed the best of Churchill's writings. Pattee noted that *Richard Carvel, The Crossing*, and *The Crisis* "survive and doubtless will survive. . . . They are more than mere romances: they are interpretations of America and Americanism."[11] Arthur Hobson

Quinn gave Churchill six pages in his historical survey, *American Fiction,* first published in 1936. But Quinn's treatment consisted largely of summaries of the plots of the novels, and he also stressed the historical romances as the most lasting Churchill contributions to American fiction.[12]

By World War II, Churchill was scarcely considered in literary histories at all. The *Literary History of the United States* (1946) mentions him only three times in commenting about other authors or literary issues;[13] there is no separate treatment of him, even as a minor figure. *The Literature of the American People,* a work in the authorship of which Quinn shared, has no discussion of his works beyond the comment that "his historical romances like well-executed mural paintings are heroic and ultrapatriotic in spirit. His early books at least are characterized by painstaking craftsmanship."[14] In the main, Churchill is no longer mentioned in literary histories; if he is, he receives only passing attention as a representative of historical fiction.

What, then, is Churchill's value for today's student? The answer lies not altogether in the realm of the early historical romances, though these have proved to be the books with some lasting popularity. *Richard Carvel, The Crisis,* and *The Crossing* are accurate in their epic portrayals of the nation's past. Despite sentimental plot structures and flimsy character portrayal which seriously detract from their literary worth, they still afford exciting avenues for adult lay readers to learn of the earlier eras in American history. And they remain excellent as fiction for younger readers.

But the scholar and literary historian will find Churchill's later work more rewarding. For in the political and problem novels Churchill is also an historian—an historian of another subject. Here he recorded, in infallible tones, the interests and preoccupations of the Progressive mind of the Theodore Roosevelt vintage and era.[15] The early Progressive advocacy of the ideals of the Fathers; the attack on business concentration and trusts; the emphasis on a social gospel; the reliance on the ways of science; and the more specific Progressive Party reforms of initiative and referendum, women's suffrage, direct primaries, popular election of senators, the eight-hour day, and immigration restriction—all are serious or lesser preoccupations of the Churchill novels after 1904.

Vernon Parrington spoke of Churchill as the writer most representative of the spirit of Progressivism, and E. H. Eby records that Parrington considered Churchill, Robert Herrick, and Jack London important writers "because they were in touch with deep currents of American thought."[16] Though Parrington is somewhat out of critical favor at the moment, his judgment of Churchill still holds. Seldom a deep or original thinker in his novels, never a literary leader, Churchill was a man of high ideals and integrity who was representative of prevailing middle-class thought. As Carl Van Doren noted, he was "a sort of unconscious politician among novelists, [gathering] his premonitions at happy moments when the drift is already setting in."[17]

No less than eight Churchill novels stood among the top best-sellers between 1899 and 1915; five led the lists in the number one position for their years. Only two works of fiction, *The Celebrity* and *The Dwelling-Place of Light,* failed to make the very top bracket in sales. Few authors before or since could boast as much. That this tremendous popularity brought Churchill fame and wealth is not so important as that it made him the mirror of public taste for sixteen years. It is as such that his value survives today. When the scholar of the American scene searches for a guide to the Progressive mind of the early years of the twentieth century, he can do no better than to open the pages of Winston Churchill, novelist, historian, politician, preacher—and, above all, American.

Notes and References

Chapter One

1. Winston S. Churchill, *A Roving Commission* (New York, 1941), p. 219.
2. "Winston Churchill," *Book News*, LVII (August, 1899), 665-66.
3. Quoted in St. Louis *Globe-Democrat*, March 23, 1938, p. 2.
4. Quoted in St. Louis *Post-Dispatch*, Nov. 19, 1899, p. 39.
5. Churchill later told an interviewer: "Paul Jones was always one of my great boyhood heroes, and I presume that had something to do with my going to Annapolis." (See Joe Mitchell Chapple, "A Day With the Author of *Richard Carvel*," *National Magazine*, XI [December, 1899], 252.)
6. Register No. 4460, Naval Academy Records, Navy Section, U. S. National Archives, Washington, D. C.
7. *Ibid.*
8. "The only reason he ever gave for his determination to leave the Navy after he graduated at Annapolis was to gratify his ambition to become an author," James Gazzam told the St. Louis *Post-Dispatch* in 1899. (St. Louis *Post-Dispatch*, *loc. cit.*)
9. Boston *Herald*, Aug. 27, 1899, p. 30.
10. "Winston Churchill," *Book News*, *loc. cit.*
11. W. McAdoo, Acting Secretary of the Navy, to Churchill, Aug. 6, 1894; copy in Navy Section, U. S. National Archives, Washington, D. C.
12. J. M. Dixon, "Real Persons and Places in 'The Crisis'," *Bookman*, XIV (September, 1901), 17.
13. Churchill acknowledged his debt by dedicating *The Celebrity* to Albert Shaw.
14. Chapple, p. 250.
15. "Interesting People: George P. Brett," *American Magazine*, LXXI (March, 1911), 601.
16. From an interview Churchill granted Mrs. Phoebe G. Storms in the summer of 1931; quoted in her unpublished M.A. thesis, *Winston Churchill: A Critical Study*, Southern Methodist University, June, 1941.
17. Fred Lewis Pattee, *The New American Literature* (New York, 1930), p. 59.

18. *The Celebrity* (New York, 1899), p. 6.

19. *Ibid.*, p. 302.

20. Van Wyck Brooks, *The Confident Years, 1885-1915* (New York, 1955), p. 100.

21. *Ibid.*, p. 105.

22. *The Celebrity*, p. 169.

23. Quoted in St. Louis *Globe-Democrat*, Dec. 8, 1899, p. 14. At least one reader failed to see the humor. Henry James remarked that "the action moves in an air . . . in which everyone, and most of all Mr. Churchill, is so desperately sly, so bewilderingly crushing, and so unfathomably clever at his [the "Celebrity's"] expense that we are induced to saying we should doubtless enjoy the joke if we only knew what it is about." (Leon Edel, ed., *The American Essays of Henry James* [New York, 1956], pp. 217-18.)

Chapter Two

1. Fred L. Pattee reports, "In a history class at the Naval Academy he awakened to his life-work." This may be an exaggeration since the official record does not show that he took any history courses at Annapolis. It is possible, of course, that American history may have been an unrecorded "extra" in the Naval Cadet's training of that day. (Pattee, *The New American Literature*, p. 94.)

2. St. Louis *Post-Dispatch, loc. cit.*

3. Boston *Herald, loc. cit.*

4. "Admiral Dewey: A Character Sketch," *Review of Reviews,* XVII (June, 1898), 676-88.

5. "By Order of the Admiral: A Story of the Times," *Century,* LVI (July, 1898), 341.

6. *Ibid.*, p. 326.

7. *Ibid.*, p. 334.

8. "Battle with Cervera's Fleet Off Santiago," *Review of Reviews,* XVIII (August, 1898), 153-67.

9. Frank L. Mott, *Golden Multitudes* (New York, 1947), p. 207.

10. Carl Van Doren, *The American Novel, 1789-1939* (New York, 1949), p. 216.

11. George Washington was enshrined in a number of novels that appeared in the 1890's. Among them were George Morgan's *John Littleton of J.*, Adelaide Skeel's and William Bearley's *King Washington, A Romance of the Hudson*, Mrs. Burton Harrison's *A Son of the Old Dominion*, Hubert Fuller's *Vivian of Old Virginia*, and Pauline Mackie's *Mademoiselle de Berny: A Story of Valley Forge.*

12. Boston *Herald, loc. cit.*

13. *Richard Carvel* (New York, 1899), p. 25.

14. Some critics did an injustice to Churchill by suggesting that in *Richard Carvel* he had tried to imitate Mitchell's success. (See "Hugh Wynne in Court Dress," *The Book Buyer*, XIX [1899], 372.) Actually, Churchill was working on his novel many months before *Hugh Wynne* appeared.

15. "Winston Churchill," *Book News, loc. cit.*

16. *Book Reviews*, New York, February, 1900.

17. Mott, p. 312.

18. George Brett, Jr. told me in 1955 that the American Macmillan editions alone had hit the 800,000 mark.

19. Among the favorable reviews were those in the *Atlantic Monthly, Review of Reviews,* the *Dial,* the *Nation,* the *Critic,* and the New York *Times.*

20. Boston *Herald, loc. cit.*

21. Some observers thought Churchill was a worthy prospect for the kailyard school of writers. Public interest in John Paul Jones, partly fostered by Churchill's *Richard Carvel,* caused the American State Department to make inquiries about the naval hero's burial place in Paris. After considerable investigation, it was discovered that Jones's unmarked grave lay in an unkempt part of a French burial yard. The United States government financed the transfer of the remains to this country, where they were buried in the chapel of the Naval Academy at Annapolis. Prominent newspaper stories in 1899 gave Churchill full credit for instigating this revival of interest in a neglected Revolutionary hero.

22. Charles C. Walcutt, *The Romantic Compromise in the Novels of Winston Churchill,* University of Michigan Contributions in Modern Philology, No. 18 (Ann Arbor, 1951), p. 9.

23. Boston *Herald, loc. cit.*

24. See Winston S. Churchill, *A Roving Commission,* p. 217, for the correspondence of the two men. Other reports of this incident have held that the Englishman suggested the American should change his name—to which the American is said to have replied that, since he was three years older than the English Churchill, he felt he had the right to keep the name unchallenged. (See Phil Stong, "Missouri," *Holiday, XIV* [November, 1953], 112.)

25. Chapple, p. 248.

26. Interview in New York *Commercial Advertiser,* Sept. 15, 1899, p. 10.

27. Pattee, *The New American Literature,* p. 94.

28. Quoted in Chapple, p. 249.

29. *The Crisis* (New York, 1901), pp. 11-12.

30. Elisha Brent was patterned after a Captain John Boffinger, who also gave Churchill his account of the origin of the words "texas"

and "stateroom" (*The Crisis,* pp. 324-25). Mark Twain objected to these etymologies Churchill had advanced. (See "Two Etymologies," *Word Study,* [November, 1933], pp. 5-7, for the correspondence between Twain and the G. C. Merriam Company, and Churchill and the Merriam Company.)

31. Mott lists *The Crisis* as a best-seller for 1900, an obvious error in date, since the book was not published until 1901 (Mott, p. 312). Alice Payne Hackett reports that it was on the *Bookman* list and *Publisher's Weekly* résumé as the top seller of 1901. (Alice Payne Hackett, *Fifty Years of Best Sellers, 1895-1945* [New York, 1945], p. 17.)

32. Philadelphia *North American,* June 10, 1901, p. 11.

33. Ernest E. Leisy, *The American Historical Novel* (Norman, Okla., 1950), p. 160. Churchill made one historical mistake in depicting a premature Republican reverence for Lincoln before 1860.

34. *Saturday Evening Post,* Sept. 14, 1901, p. 4.

35. "How to Write a Popular Novel," Boston *Herald,* Oct. 19, 1902, magazine section, p. 3.

36. *The Crisis,* p. 36.

37. *Ibid.,* p. 171.

38. Firmin Dredd in *Bookman,* XIII (June, 1901), 345-47. *Bookman* also pointed out the anachronisms in *The Crisis* in two articles that appeared in December, 1901, and in January, 1902.

39. St. Louis *Post-Dispatch,* Jan. 25, 1903, magazine section, p. 6.

40. New York *Times,* Oct. 5, 1901, "Saturday Review of Books and Art," p. 690.

41. Part I of the book, "The Borderland," was completed for serialization in *Collier's* magazine in the fall of 1903.

42. *The Crossing* (New York, 1904), p. 597.

43. *Ibid.,* p. 326.

44. *Ibid.,* p. 579.

45. *Ibid.,* p. 594.

46. Pattee, *The New American Literature,* p. 97.

47. *Critic,* XLV (August, 1904), 188.

48. A. E. Hancock, "The Historical Fiction of Winston Churchill," *Outlook,* LXXVII (July 30, 1904), 755.

49. Herbert Croly, "Some Really Historical Novels," *The Lamp,* XXVI (July, 1903), 509.

50. See Warren I. Titus, ed., "The Senator and the Author," *Indiana Magazine of History,* LV (June, 1959), 170.

51. Henry Steele Commager, "Creating a New Nation; based on *The Crossing,*" *Scholastic,* LV (Nov. 9, 1949), 12-13.

Chapter Three

1. Lisle Abbott Rose, *A Survey of American Economic Fiction, 1902-1909*, abstract of University of Chicago dissertation (Chicago, 1938), pp. 4, 6.
2. Pattee, *The New American Literature*, pp. 106, 107.
3. Henry F. Pringle, *Theodore Roosevelt*, Harvest Book Edition (New York, 1956), p. 345.
4. Richard Hofstadter, *The American Political Tradition* (New York, 1949), p. 207.
5. Boston *Herald*, Aug. 12, 1906, p. 1.
6. The Boston *Herald* sent a special reporter to follow the Churchill campaign and featured on its front page the speeches and accusations he made against the railroad. Other newspapers supporting Churchill's candidacy were the New York *Tribune*, New York *Times*, New York *Herald*, New York *Evening Post*, New York *American and World*, Boston *American*, Philadelphia *Ledger and North American*, and the Chicago *Tribune*. *Collier's Weekly* had an article by Mark Sullivan on the New Hampshire situation (Aug. 7, 1906); *Review of Reviews* had a similar feature called "Churchill and New Hampshire" (August, 1906).
7. For a more detailed account of the convention and the ensuing campaign, see Leon B. Richardson, *William E. Chandler: Republican* (New York, 1940), p. 677.
8. "Churchill's Virtual Victory," *Outlook*, LXXXIV (Sept. 29, 1906), 243.
9. Like Roosevelt, Churchill had moved further to the left by 1912. In his speeches, he advocated women's suffrage, recall of judicial decisions, easier amendment to the Constitution, social welfare legislation for women and children, laws for a minimum wage and an eight-hour day, workman's compensation, health insurance in industry, conservation, more primary election laws, and ratification of the sixteenth and seventeenth amendments to the Constitution. Churchill pitched his campaign very much from a national standpoint since progressive forces already had control of the executive branch and the legislature in New Hampshire.
10. "Harlakenden House" was the summer residence of Wilson in 1913 and 1914. Mrs. Wilson, in particular, was enthusiastic in her liking for the Cornish summers.
11. *Coniston* (New York, 1906), p. 12.
12. *Ibid.*, p. 67.
13. *Ibid.*, p. 79.
14. *Ibid.*, p. 510.

15. *Ibid.*, p. 515.

16. *Ibid.*, p. 540.

17. Hackett, p. 22. Another "propaganda novel," Upton Sinclair's *The Jungle*, was sixth on the list for 1906.

18. *Atlantic Monthly*, XCIX (January, 1907), 123; *North American Review*, CLXXXIII (Sept. 7, 1906), 415-17; *Review of Reviews*, XXXIV (August, 1906), 256.

19. *Harper's Weekly*, L (Aug. 4, 1906), 1110.

20. Concord *Daily Patriot*, June 20, 1906, p. 13. Churchill had already met Bryce in England. When the Englishman became ambassador to the United States in 1907, he was a frequent visitor at "Harlakenden House."

21. Alfred Kazin, *On Native Grounds* (New York, 1942), p. 109.

22. *Coniston*, pp. 542-43.

23. *Ibid.*, p. 542.

24. Fred L. Pattee, *Penn State Yankee* (State College, Pa., 1953), p. 40.

25. *Coniston*, p. 8.

26. Coniston is actually Croydon, N. H.; Brampton is Newport; Harwich, Claremont; Clovelly, Cornish. Coniston Water is the Sugar River; Truro County is Sullivan County; and Coniston Mountain is probably Mount Ascutney on the Vermont-New Hampshire border. Of course, Concord is the "State Capital" of the novel, and its Eagle Hotel becomes the Pelican House in *Coniston*. Thus did Churchill use the familiar scenes around him.

27. *Coniston*, p. 1.

28. Morris E. Speare, *The Political Novel, Its Development in England and in America* (New York, 1924), p. 311.

29. Quoted in Storms thesis, p. 132.

30. *Mr. Crewe's Career* (New York, 1908), p. 263.

31. Stanley Johnson, in an article for *World's Work*, gave Churchill all the credit for forcing these New Hampshire suits. (See Stanley Johnson, "The Novelist and His Novels in Politics," *World's Work*, XVII [December, 1908], 11016-20.)

32. Churchill himself had gained the support of great numbers of women in his campaign of 1906.

33. Many readers thought Hilary Vane was a fictional portrait of Frank Streeter, the Boston and Maine Railroad attorney in Concord who finally left the railroad and joined the reform element of the Republican Party.

34. *Dial*, XLIV (June 1, 1908), 349; *Independent*, LXIV (June 19, 1908), 1400.

35. *Mr. Crewe's Career*, p. 182.

36. Richard Hofstadter, *The Age of Reform* (New York, 1955), p. 195.

Chapter Four

1. James H. Barnett found that the greatest number of articles on divorce appeared in American magazines between 1905 and 1914; there was a gradual decline after that, with a new increase from 1928 to 1932, though the second peak did not match the first. (James H. Barnett, *Divorce and the American Divorce Novel, 1858-1937* [Philadelphia, 1939], p. 34.)

2. This alienation because of questionable business practices reminds one of Bartley Hubbard and Marcia Gaylord in Howells' *A Modern Instance*. The titles of the two books are also strikingly similar.

3. The phrase is from Walcutt.

4. Frank L. Mott lists it as a "better seller" for 1910. (Mott, p. 325.) Alice Payne Hackett reports that it was second on the *Bookman* lists for the year. (Hackett, p. 26.)

5. *Nation*, XC (March 21, 1910), 318.

6. *Outlook*, XCIV (April 23, 1910), 956.

7. *Dial*, XLVIII (June 1, 1910), 396.

8. *Bookman*, XXXI (May, 1910), 308.

9. *A Modern Chronicle* (New York, 1910), p. 173.

10. *Ibid.*, p. 216.

11. "A Matter for the Individual to Settle," *Hearst's Magazine: The World Today*, XXI (June, 1912), 2395.

12. "Our 'Common Sense' Marriages," *Good Housekeeping*, LVII (July, 1913), 55.

13. *Ibid.*, p. 59.

14. Grant C. Knight, *The Strenuous Age in American Literature* (Chapel Hill, 1954), p. 198.

15. Honora Leffingwell's greatest fault, in the mind of the former President, must have been her failure to have any children by either of her marriages.

Chapter Five

1. Ralph H. Gabriel, *The Course of American Democratic Thought* (New York, 1940), p. 332.

2. Churchill knew Episcopal Bishop Edward L. Parker of Concord, New Hampshire, very well. He was also well acquainted with a number of other Episcopal church leaders.

3. Mott, p. 226. Mott says "one cannot dip into the popular literature of the first two decades of the twentieth century without being impressed by the emphasis on the church and its problems."

4. "Modern Government and Christianity," *Atlantic Monthly,* CIX (January, 1912), 18.

5. "Winston Churchill's Christian Anarchism," *Current Literature,* LII (February, 1912), 196-98.

6. *The Inside of the Cup* (New York, 1913), p. 167.

7. This scene reminds one of Austen Vane's final denunciation of Augustus Flint in *Mr. Crewe's Career.*

8. Hackett, p. 30.

9. *Nation,* XCVI (June 12, 1913), 598.

10. *Dial,* LV (Sept. 1, 1913), 147.

11. *Catholic World,* XCVIII (October, 1913), 113. Churchill's novel probably offended Catholics and fundamentalists most of all. *America,* a Roman Catholic weekly, said the book was "an object lesson in the mental and moral chaos to which Protestantism reduces the cleverest writers who are guided by its principles." (Quoted in "Winston Churchill, Reformer," *Current Opinion,* LV [August, 1913], 123.)

12. *Churchman,* CVIII (July, 1913), 290.

13. *Athenaeum,* June 7, 1913, p. 620; *Spectator,* June 21, 1913, p. 1065.

14. Though Churchill's ideas remarkably parallel many of Bellamy's, I have been unable to find that he was directly influenced by the earlier writer.

15. *Atlantic,* CXII (November, 1913), 700.

16. Quoted in *The Inside of the Cup,* p. 277.

17. Reviewing the book in 1955, Clarence Gohdes said: ". . . . as a discussion of emancipation from rigid orthodoxy it still has a little warmth. All told, isn't it as good—or as bad—as Sinclair Lewis's *Elmer Gantry?*" (*Georgia Review,* IX [Spring, 1955], 113.)

18. Churchill told Mrs. Phoebe Storms, "I was often asked if I did not intend to go into the church; I could perhaps imagine myself as a clergyman." (Quoted in Storms thesis, *loc. cit.*)

19. "The Modern Quest for a Religion," *Century,* LXXXVII (December, 1913), 169. (Many requests, especially from clergymen, led *Literary Digest* to publish a summary of this article in its issue for Dec. 27, 1913, pp. 1278-79.)

20. Charles Walcutt has found elements of American transcendentalism in *The Inside of the Cup.* "Here in Christian terms is the

doctrine of American transcendentalism, with its special element of democratic idealism" (Walcutt, p. 29n.). Churchill mentions Emerson in several of his novels.

Chapter Six

1. Quoted in Storms thesis, pp. 197-98.
2. From a *Hearst's* magazine advertisement.
3. *Dial,* LIX (July 15, 1915), 63.
4. *Nation,* C (June 24, 1915), 711.
5. *Bookman,* XLI (July, 1915), 555.
6. New York *Times,* June 6, 1915, p. 209.
7. Roosevelt to Churchill, August 4, 1915. Reprinted in Elting E. Morison, ed., *The Letters of Theodore Roosevelt,* VIII (Cambridge, 1954), 958-59.
8. "Roosevelt and His Friends," *Collier's* LVII (July 8, 1916), 15.
9. "A Plea for the American Tradition," *Harper's,* CXXXII (January, 1916), 252.
10. Mott, *op. cit.;* James D. Hart, *The Popular Book* (New York, 1950). Hart does say that Churchill was still a leading author in 1915, along with Tarkington, Gene Stratton Porter, and Zane Grey (p. 224).
11. Hackett, *op. cit.*
12. *Outlook,* CXVII (Nov. 7, 1917), 386.
13. *Independent,* XCII (Nov. 24, 1917), 385.
14. *Catholic World,* CVI (February, 1918), 694; New York *Call,* Dec. 15, 1917, p. 18.
15. H. W. Boynton, "A Stroll Through the Fair of Fiction," *Bookman,* XLVI (November, 1917), 339.
16. *Nation,* CV (Nov. 29, 1917), 600.
17. *New Republic,* XII (Oct. 13, 1917), 306.
18. Walcutt, p. 45.

Chapter Seven

1. "A Call for the Marine Corps," New York *Times,* June 14, 1917, p. 10.
2. "Naval Organization, American and British," *Atlantic,* CXX (August, 1917), 277.
3. The articles appeared in *Scribner's* for February, March, and April of 1918. They were given prominent display.
4. *A Traveller in War-Time: With an Essay on the American Contribution and the Democratic Idea* (New York, 1918), p. 116.
5. One might have thought that his 1912 experience would have disillusioned him with third-party efforts.

6. "St. Louis After the War," pamphlet by the City Plan Commission, with an Introduction by Winston Churchill (St. Louis, 1918), p. 7.

7. *Dr. Jonathan* (New York, 1919), p. 80.

8. Churchill did work with another novel during 1919 and 1920. Called *The Green Bay Tree,* it strenuously attacked money-mad magnates and radical European-imported ideals in the United States. In 1920 Macmillan printed a publisher's dummy of this novel that included six pages of chapter one, but the complete work was never published. Oddly, four years later, in 1924, Louis Bromfield was to deal with American industrialism and its effects in his first novel, *The Green Bay Tree.*

9. Kenneth W. Cameron, "Novelist Winston Churchill and the Episcopal Church," *Historiographer of the Episcopal Diocese of Connecticut,* No. 9 (October, 1954), p. 6. This article reproduces the Churchill letter to Bishop Parker of April 7, 1917.

10. "Two Minds for One," New York *Times Book Review and Magazine,* March 26, 1922, p. 3.

11. "The Knowledge of Good and Evil," *North American Review,* CCXV (April, 1922), 486.

12. *Ibid.,* p. 488.

13. Storms thesis, p. 8.

14. Cyril Clemens, "A Visit With the American Winston Churchill," *Hobbies,* LII (May, 1947), 145.

15. "Book Prices Stir Winston Churchill," New York *Times,* Dec. 3, 1925, p. 3.

16. "Offers to Publish Churchill Books at One Dollar," New York *Times,* Dec. 5, 1925, p. 27.

17. "They Say," New York *Times,* Aug. 10, 1930, sec. 9, p. 2.

18. *The Uncharted Way; the Psychology of the Gospel Doctrine* (Philadelphia, 1940), p. 138.

19. *Ibid.,* p. 251.

20. Quoted in Storms thesis, p. 270.

21. The book was published by Dorrance in Philadelphia, not by Churchill's old publisher the Macmillan Company.

22. "Books," New York *Herald-Tribune,* July 14, 1940, sec. 9, p. 8.

23. *Christian Century,* LVII (May 29, 1940), 706.

24. *Time,* XXXV (June 17, 1940), 88.

25. Clemens, *loc. cit.*

26. Asa Don Dickinson, *One Thousand Best Books* (New York, 1931), p. 62.

27. New York *Times,* March 13, 1947, p. 27.

28. New York *Herald-Tribune,* March 14, 1947, p. 20.

Chapter Eight

1. Clemens, *loc. cit.*
2. Upton Sinclair reports that by 1927 Churchill "had become a complete mystic." (See Upton Sinclair, *My Lifetime in Letters* [Columbia, Missouri, 1960], p. 135.)
3. Arthur Link has recently written that "progressivism was certainly on the downgrade if not in decay after 1918." In suggesting some reasons for this decline, he says: ". . . the progressive coalition of 1916 was inherently unstable. Indeed, it was so wracked by inner tensions that it could not survive, and destruction came inexorably, it seemed systematically, from 1917 to 1920. . . . The major objectives of the progressive movement of the prewar years had in fact been largely achieved by 1920. . . . the intellectual-political climate of the 1920's was vastly different from the one that had prevailed in the preceding two decades." (Arthur S. Link, "What Happened to the Progressive Movement in the 1920's?" *American Historical Review,* LXIV [July, 1959], 838, 841, 844.) To be sure, the Progressive Robert La Follette made his strongest bid for the Presidency in 1924, but La Follette did not represent the same brand of Progressivism that Theodore Roosevelt and the early Churchill had stood for. The Bull Moose nomination of 1912 had proved this.
4. John Chamberlain, *Farewell to Reform* (New York, 1932).
5. "Where Are the Pre-War Radicals?" *Survey Graphic,* LV (Feb. 1, 1926), 556-66.
6. Speaking for American novelists, Churchill had paid high tribute to William Dean Howells on the occasion of Howells' seventy-fifth birthday dinner: "Perhaps not the least of the debts which literature owes him [Howells] is that he has kept himself clean against the pollution of American letters by the muddy tide of commercialism, of materialism, which has swept over our country, and which is leaving its stain on other dignified professions besides our own." (*Harper's Weekly,* LVI [Mar. 9, 1912], 27.)
7. *Richard Carvel* (New York, 1914), p. x.
8. John C. Underwood, *Literature and Insurgency* (New York, 1914), p. 315.
9. Carl Van Doren, *Contemporary American Novelists, 1900-1920* (New York, 1922), p. 56.
10. Carl Van Doren, *The American Novel* (New York, 1940), p. 261. Long before this, in 1924, H. L. Mencken could claim the gift of prophecy when he wrote, "Back in 1908 I predicted the destruction of Upton Sinclair the artist by Upton Sinclair the visionary and reformer. Sinclair's bones now bleach upon the beach. Beside them repose those of many another man and woman of great promise—for

example, Winston Churchill." (H. L. Mencken, *Prejudices, Fourth Series* [New York, 1924], p. 292.)

11. Pattee, *The New American Literature*, pp. 93, 95.

12. Arthur Hobson Quinn, *American Fiction, An Historical and Critical Survey* (New York, 1936), pp. 496-501.

13. Robert Spiller, *et al.*, *Literary History of the United States* (New York, 1946), pp. 610, 1118, 1122.

14. Arthur H. Quinn, *et al.*, *The Literature of the American People* (New York, 1951), p. 890.

15. In a letter to me, Dec. 1, 1955, Upton Sinclair declared of Churchill: "His novels were propaganda, like most of mine, but he had great influence in his time."

16. Vernon L. Parrington, *Main Currents in American Thought*, III (New York, 1930), 348, xiv.

17. Van Doren, *Contemporary American Novelists*, p. 51.

Selected Bibliography

PRIMARY SOURCES

Books and Plays by Churchill

The Celebrity; An Episode. New York: Macmillan, 1898.
Coniston. New York: Macmillan, 1906.
The Crisis. New York: Macmillan, 1901.
The Crisis: A Play in Four Acts. New York: Samuel French, 1927.
The Crossing. New York: Macmillan, 1904.
Dr. Jonathan: A Play in Three Acts. New York: Macmillan, 1919.
The Dwelling-Place of Light. New York: Macmillan, 1917.
The Faith of Frances Craniford. New York: The Episcopal Church
    Pension Fund, 1917.
A Far Country. New York: Macmillan, 1915.
The Inside of the Cup. New York: Macmillan, 1913.
Mr. Crewe's Career. New York: Macmillan, 1908.
Mr. Keegan's Elopement. New York: Macmillan, 1903.
A Modern Chronicle. New York: Macmillan, 1910.
Richard Carvel. New York: Macmillan, 1899.
The Title-Mart: A Comedy in Three Acts. New York: Macmillan, 1905.
*A Traveller in War-Time; With an Essay on the American Contribu-
    tion and the Democratic Idea.* New York: Macmillan, 1918.
The Uncharted Way: The Psychology of the Gospel Doctrine.
    Philadelphia: Dorrance & Company, 1940.

Other Writings

"Admiral Dewey: A Character Sketch," *Review of Reviews,* XVII
    (June, 1898), 676-88.
"An Appreciation of Crater Lake National Park," pamphlet published
    by U.S. Railroad Administration, National Park Series (July,
    1919).
"The Author and His Critic," *Bookman,* IX (July, 1899), 403-5.
"Battle With Cervera's Fleet Off Santiago," *Review of Reviews,*
    XVIII (August, 1898), 153-67.
"By Order of the Admiral: A Story of the Times," *Century,* LVI
    (July, 1898), 323-41.
"A Call for the Marine Corps," New York *Times,* XXII (June 14,
    1917), 10.

"Free Passes As Retaining Fees," pamphlet published by Boston Herald Company, 1906.

"Glory of the States: New Hampshire," *American Magazine,* LXXXII (September, 1916), 37.

"Interesting People: George P. Brett," *American Magazine,* LXXI (March, 1911), 601-2.

"The Knowledge of Good and Evil," *North American Review,* CCXV (April, 1922), 483-500.

"A Matter For the Individual to Settle," *Hearst's Magazine: The World Today,* XXI (June, 1912), 2395.

"Modern Government and Christianity," *Atlantic,* CIX (January, 1912), 12-22.

"The Modern Quest for a Religion," *Century,* LXXXVII (December, 1913), 169-74.

"Naval Organization, American and British," *Atlantic,* CXX (August, 1917), 277-84.

"On the Wilderness Trail," *Current Literature,* XXXVII (July, 1904), 38-41.

"Our Common Sense Marriages," *Good Housekeeping,* LVII (July, 1913), 53-59.

"A Plea For the American Tradition," *Harper's,* CXXXII (January, 1916), 249-56.

"Proportion of Fiction and History in My New Novel," New York *Journal,* May 25, 1901.

"Roosevelt and His Friends," *Collier's,* LVII (July 8, 1916), 15.

"Rose Light Lingered On the Hill: A Poem," *Century,* LXIII (March, 1902), 738.

"A Sonnet," *Collier's,* XLIV (January 1, 1910), 8.

"The Supreme Question Facing Our City and Country Today," *American City,* XX (January, 1919), 1-5.

"To the Men and Women of New Hampshire: An Open Letter," pamphlet published by Ruemely Press, Concord, N. H., 1912.

"A Tryst," *Scribner's Magazine,* XXXI (February, 1902), 144.

"Two Minds for One," New York *Times Book Review and Magazine,* XXVII (March 26, 1922), 3.

"An Uncharted Way," *Yale Review,* XI (April, 1922), 526-45.

SECONDARY SOURCES

BALDWIN, CHARLES C. *The Men Who Make Our Novels.* New York: Moffat, Yard and Co., 1919. A very brief chapter on Churchill that gives mostly the known biographical facts of his life.

BARRON, LEONARD. "The Summer White House," *Country Life,* XXIV

(July, 1913), 90. An account of Woodrow Wilson at "Harlakenden House."

BLOTNER, JOSEPH L. *The Political Novel.* Doubleday Short Studies in Political Science. Garden City, N. Y.: Doubleday and Co., 1955. Brief consideration of *Coniston* and *Mr. Crewe's Career* as part of a larger examination of the genre in English, American, and Continental literature.

CAMERON, KENNETH W. "Novelist Winston Churchill and the Episcopal Church," *Historiographer of the Episcopal Diocese of Connecticut*, No. 9 (October, 1954), pp. 6-7.

CHAPPLE, JOE MITCHELL. "A Day With the Author of 'Richard Carvel'," *National Magazine*, XI (December, 1899), 247-52. One of the many early articles that treated Churchill as a national celebrity. Recounts a visit to his home in New Hampshire.

"CHURCHILL AND NEW HAMPSHIRE," *Review of Reviews*, XXXIV (August, 1906), 142-43. An account of Churchill's campaign to win the Republican gubernatorial nomination in 1906.

"CHURCHILL'S EXPOSURES ARE OF NATIONAL CONCERN," *Arena*, XXXVI (October, 1906), 410-14. An account of Churchill's attack on Boston and Maine Railroad domination of New Hampshire state politics.

"CHURCHILL'S VIRTUAL VICTORY," *Outlook*, LXXXIV (September 29, 1906), 243. How most of Churchill's reforms were carried over into the 1906 Republican platform in New Hampshire. Overly optimistic outlook.

CLEMENS, CYRIL. "A Visit with the American Winston Churchill," *Hobbies*, LII (May, 1947), 144-45. An interview granted during Churchill's last visit to St. Louis.

COOPER, FREDERIC T. "Some Representative American Story Tellers: XII—W. Churchill," *Bookman*, XXXI (May, 1910), 246-53. Also reprinted in *Some American Story Tellers.* New York: Henry Holt and Co., 1911. Calls Churchill a careful constructor of the old-fashioned novel who patterns his work on mid-Victorian models. Feels plot construction is his principal weakness. "Every reason to believe that his best and biggest work is yet to come." Still a valuable critique.

DIXON, J. M. "Real Persons and Places in 'The Crisis'," *Bookman*, XIV (September, 1901), 17-20.

ELLIS, J. BRECKENRIDGE. "Missourians Abroad—No. 11, Winston Churchill," *Missouri Historical Review*, XVI (July, 1922), 517. An appreciation of a favorite son of Missouri. Finds his main contribution to literature is in the field of history.

FOLLETT, WILSON. "The Novelist's Use of History," *Bookman*, LXVIII (February, 1928), 156-62.

GILDER, JEANETTE. "The American Historical Novelists," *Independent*, LIII (September 5, 1901), 2096-2102.

GRIFFIN, LLOYD W. "Winston Churchill, American Novelist," *More Books* (Bulletin of the Boston Public Library), XXIII (November, 1948), 331-38. Views Churchill as a neglected novelist. Summaries of all the novels with principal emphasis on the early historical works. No criticism.

HANCOCK, A. E. "The Historical Fiction of Winston Churchill," *Outlook*, LXXVII (July 30, 1904), 753-55. Essentially a review of *The Crossing* that sees Churchill's genius in creating panoramic background effect, not individual character delineation or plot.

HART, IRVING. "The Most Popular Authors of Fiction Between 1900 and 1925," *Publisher's Weekly*, CVII (February 21, 1925), 619-21. Shows Churchill's enormous popularity during these years.

HART, JAMES D. *The Popular Book*. New York: Oxford University Press, 1950. A study of popular reading tastes in America.

HICKS, GRANVILLE. *The Great Tradition: An Interpretation of American Literature Since the Civil War*. New York: Macmillan, 1935. A Marxist-oriented study. A very brief treatment of Churchill in a chapter on the muckrakers. Contains one piece of factual misinformation: "*A Modern Chronicle* depicts the political maneuvers of a railroad."

HOFSTADTER, RICHARD. *The Age of Reform*. New York: Alfred A. Knopf, 1955. A good study of the political climate of the Progressive era.

HOFSTADTER, RICHARD AND BEATRICE. "Winston Churchill: A Study in the Popular Novel," *American Quarterly*, II (Spring 1950), 12-28. A perceptive examination of the reasons for Churchill's popularity.

IRVIN, FREDERIC B. *The Didacticism of Winston Churchill*. Unpublished doctoral dissertation, University of Pittsburgh, 1947.

JOHNSON, STANLEY. "The Novelist and His Novels in Politics," *World's Work*, XVII (December, 1908), 11016-20. Traces the origins of *Coniston* and *Mr. Crewe's Career*.

KILLAT, JOHANNES. *Das Amerikabild des Romanschriftstellers Winston Churchill*. Berlin: Junker and Dunnhaupt, 1940. A doctor's dissertation that is an unpretentious compendium of information about the progressive America of Churchill's day. Remarkably well-informed on American history, but not so good in interpreting Churchill. Almost claims Churchill as a fellow Nazi.

KNIGHT, GRANT C. *The Strenuous Age in American Literature*. Chapel Hill: University of North Carolina Press, 1954. Interesting, informative study of the first decade of the twentieth century.

Selected Bibliography

MACFARLANE, PETER C. "Evolution of a Novelist," *Collier's*, LII
(December 27, 1913), 5-6. A good article, largely biographical,
that tells how and why Churchill moved from romance to
"realism."
MOTT, FRANK L. *Golden Multitudes*. New York: Macmillan, 1947.
A study of best-sellers in American literary history.
PARRINGTON, VERNON L. *Main Currents in American Thought*. Vol.
III. New York: Harcourt, Brace and Company, 1927. Valuable
notes from a section of a lecture on "The Problem Novel and the
Diversion from Naturalism." Comments are still appropriate
and useful.
PATTEE, FRED L. *A History of American Literature Since 1870*.
New York: Century, 1915.
————. *The New American Literature, 1890-1930*. New York:
Century, 1930. A discussion of Churchill as a Waverley romancer.
PITT, WILLIAM. "Who's Who in Coniston," *Yankee* (November, 1937),
pp. 12-15.
QUINN, ARTHUR H. *American Fiction: An Historical and Critical
Survey*. New York: D. Appleton-Century Company, 1936. Five
pages of discussion of all of Churchill's novels—the longest treat-
ment in any major fictional survey. Sees Churchill's importance
only as a writer of juvenile historical fiction.
SCHNEIDER, ROBERT W. "Novelist to a Generation: The American
Winston Churchill," *Midwest Quarterly*, III (January, 1962),
149-82. Traces origins of some of Churchill's Progressive thinking.
SPEARE, MORRIS E. *The Political Novel: Its Development in England
and in America*. New York: Oxford University Press, 1924.
A useful chapter on *Coniston* and *Mr. Crewe's Career*.
SPILO, ROBERT S. *The Political Novels and Life of Winston Churchill*.
Unpublished master's thesis, New York University, 1948. Deals
only with the political phase.
STORMS, PHOEBE GRACE. *Winston Churchill: A Critical Study*.
Unpublished master's thesis, Southern Methodist University,
1941. Chief value is that the author interviewed Churchill to
obtain much of her information.
TITUS, WARREN I., ed. "The Senator and the Author," *Indiana
Magazine of History*, LV (June, 1959), 169-78. An exchange
of correspondence between Senator Albert Beveridge and
Churchill that shows Beveridge's high regard for the author
both as a writer and as a political figure.
————. *Winston Churchill, American: A Critical Biography*. Un-
published doctoral dissertation, New York University, 1957.
UNDERWOOD, JOHN. *Literature and Insurgency*. New York: Mitchell
Kennerley, 1914. Chapter 7 on "Winston Churchill and Civic

Righteousness" defends the author against Frederic T. Cooper's *Bookman* article of May, 1910. Strongly eulogistic. Says Churchill's novels cannot be judged as works of fiction but as "human documents and national studies."

VAN DOREN, CARL. *Contemporary American Novelists, 1900-1920.* New York: Macmillan, 1922. Short chapter on Churchill that views him primarily as a romanticist who has refreshed the nation's memory of a tapestried past. Sees little merit in Churchill as a literary artist.

WALCUTT, CHARLES C. *The Romantic Compromise in the Novels of Winston Churchill.* Ann Arbor: University of Michigan Press, 1951. Largely reprinted in the author's *American Literary Naturalism, A Divided Stream.* Minneapolis: University of Minnesota Press, 1956. Probably the best evaluation available of Churchill's later problem novels beginning with *Coniston.* Sees Churchill as struggling to combine the older romantic element with newer Progressive outlook.

WHITELOCK, WILLIAM W. "Mr. Winston Churchill," *Critic,* LX (February, 1902), 135-41. A chatty interview with Churchill at "Harlakenden House." Good description of the home and countryside. Some Churchill comment on his historical method which was to perpetuate the national ideals.

"WINSTON CHURCHILL," *New Yorker,* XVI (June 1, 1940), 20. An amusing reminder to the American public that there were two Winston Churchills.

Index